BECOMING A MAN OF VALOR

MEN OF VALOR SERIES

BECOMING A
MAN *of* VALOR

mark r. laaser

BEACON HILL PRESS
OF KANSAS CITY

Cover Design: Brandon Hill
Interior Design: Sharon Page

Unless otherwise indicated, all Scripture quotations are taken from the *Holy Bible, New International Version®* (NIV®). Copyright © 1973, 1978, 1984 by Biblica, Inc.™ Used by permission of Zondervan. All rights reserved worldwide. www.zondervan.com.

Quotations marked KJV are from the King James Version.

Permission to quote from the following additional copyrighted versions of the Bible is acknowledged with appreciation.

The *New King James Version* (NKJV). Copyright © 1979, 1980, 1982 Thomas Nelson, Inc.

The *Holy Bible, New Living Translation* (NLT), copyright © 1996. Used by permission of Tyndale House Publishers, Inc., Wheaton, IL 60189. All rights reserved.

Library of Congress Cataloging-in-Publication Data

Laaser, Mark R.
    Becoming a man of valor / Mark R. Laaser.
        p. cm.
    Includes bibliographical references (p.   ).
    ISBN 978-0-8341-2740-1 (pbk.)
    1. Spirituality. 2. Integrity—Religious aspects—Christianity. 3. Christian life. I. Title.
    BV4501.3.L323 2011
    248.4—dc23
                                                                    2011023962

10 9 8 7 6 5 4 3 2 1

CONTENTS

ACKNOWLEDGMENTS

No one really writes a book alone. There are those who have contributed ideas, those who have reviewed ideas and content, and those who support through encouragement and prayer. That has certainly been the case for me.

First and foremost is the person who has contributed, reviewed, encouraged, and prayed the most—my wife, Debbie. We have been married for thirty-eight years. During that time she has gone through the good times and the bad and never stopped being my number one friend, companion, and soul mate. She is often way ahead of me emotionally and spiritually. She has been the main way that God has demonstrated his grace to me. It has been our ministry together helping couples survive the crisis of infidelity that has shaped and formed many of the ideas in this book series. To Debbie, I can never say thank you enough.

A great deal of inspiration has come through my work with men who struggle with infidelity and sex addiction. Each and every one of the hundreds I have worked with has taught me something. There is a smaller number who really helped shape the material in this book. Anonymity issues prevent me from recognizing them more publicly.

Several men introduced me to certain concepts in these books. I am honored to say that they are colleagues and friends. Chris Charleton first pointed me to the powerful example of the story of Nehemiah and how it reveals to us a plan for accountability. Eli Machen is a superb teacher on many subjects, and his ideas on vision are what originally influenced me about it. More recently, Greg Miller has been helping me more fully understand the value of our needing a team of people to help us heal. To all of these men I say, "Thank you very much!"

To the wonderful family of people at Beacon Hill Press of Kansas City, thank you for your confidence, faith, and trust in me. Eric Bryant originally approached me about this series, and Bonnie Perry has nurtured it along.

And in all things to God be the glory. There are times for all Christian writers, I think, when they try to simply sit at the computer, quiet their spirits, and invite God to give them insight and inspiration. I pray that all readers of these books will open themselves to this quiet place and will allow God to speak to them directly through the imperfect words, thoughts, and ideas of this series. I could not put any book out there if I did not think that God was in charge of the process.

—Mark R. Laaser
January 2011

INTRODUCTION

In this book, I want to teach you about three spiritual questions I believe we must ask ourselves every day to live a life of integrity. They shape the foundation of our Christian journey. Our answers to these questions form our character, and our character creates our behavior. Over the years I have seen the value of these questions in my own life and the lives of countless others.

Where do these questions come from? They are from the words of Jesus as found in the gospel of John. I have studied philosophy, psychology, and theology and function daily as a Christian pastoral counselor. I regularly use the skills I learned in my studies. But despite all my theological and psychological training, I return over and over to these three spiritual questions based on the words of Christ.

I've found that if all we ever studied were the interactions Jesus had with other people and the words he said to them, we would have a psychology textbook so powerful it would transform lives. I have concluded that maybe Jesus meant what he said and that maybe everything is much simpler than we make it.

We live in a complicated world—a world that many people say has lost its moral compass. Others would say that it has always been this way; we live in a "fallen" world, and today is no different. Whichever is the case, in the words of the apostle Paul, we can't conform to the ways of the world, but our mind must be transformed by the grace of God (see Rom. 12:2). The questions I want to teach you, if you answer them according to God's grace, are mind transforming.

I am a person who lost his way in a world of addiction. I have been sober now for over twenty-three years. My wife and I have had to transform our relationship. She has been an unbelievable grace. Together we have navigated the difficult road to reconciliation and forgiveness. My ability to be sober and to be a husband of integrity is based on these three questions.

My prayer is that you will find soul-transforming truth in these pages. For that to happen I encourage you to do several things. Read this book slowly; don't rush through it. In each chapter I will draw your attention to important points and provide key questions for you to ask yourself. You will get more out of the book if you take the time to answer these key questions. You may want to ask your spouse or a friend to read this book with you.

This book is the third in a series of three books I have written for Beacon Hill Press of Kansas City. The first book, *The 7 Principles of Highly Accountable Men*, will teach you how to change your life through accountability. That means, quite simply, that you will have other people in your life to encourage you. I would suggest that if you do practice accountability, you ask your accountability partners to call you regularly and ask you how you are doing with the three spiritual questions and the key questions in each chapter.

The second book in this series, *Taking Every Thought Captive,* will give you a great deal to think about on the matter of transforming your mind. Chapter 2 of that book is about meditation as a way of taking thoughts captive. You might find that some of the strategies detailed there will help you get more out of reading this book—that is, use this third book meditatively. I pray that reading this book and answering the spiritual questions in it honestly and through faith, you will lead a life of greater and greater integrity.

Before we begin, I would like to explain what I mean by integrity. The word itself comes from the Latin *integritas,*[1] which is derived from the word *integer,* meaning "whole, entire."[2] Integrity literally means being a whole person. As a Christian, I believe that wholeness is only achieved in a relationship with Christ. Belonging to Christ will guide all of us to be more like him. Knowing him gives us a definite sense of what the morality of a Christian life is really like.

Having integrity, being whole with no cracks or fissures, means we will act at all times according to our faith. In my work as a Christian pastoral counselor, I talk to my clients about being "congruent." That means their insides will match their outsides. For example, have you ever talked to a person who looks angry, sad, or anxious, but if you ask how he or she is doing, that person will say, "I'm fine." The person's outer appearance displays a certain emotion congruent with what he or she is feeling inside, but his or her words don't match. Maybe the person you are talking to is really sad, but he or she has the ability to act happy. In this case, he or she looks happy on the outside but is sad on the inside. This is not congruent and doesn't demonstrate integrity.

Integrity means that if you say you are a Christian, your attitude, appearance, words, and actions will match. Have you ever been discouraged by a person who claims to be a Christian, but his or her behavior doesn't match? The person might lie, get overly angry, be judgmental, cheat, steal, be sexually immoral, or simply unkind. There is another word we use for this kind of person. He or she is a *hypocrite,* a person who professes beliefs and opinions he or she does not hold in order to conceal his or her real feelings or motives. Hypocrisy is thus a kind of lie.

I work with addicts. Addicts are people who commit acts they have vowed to stop but can't. Addicts lie, cheat, and betray trust. Addicts who are Christian consistently amaze themselves by how unchristian their behavior can be. I find that I can't really work with addicts successfully until they grapple with and answer well the three simple questions in this book. If they can do so, becoming a sober person, a person of integrity, will be the glorious result.

To lead a life of integrity will require a person to be emotionally and spiritually mature. In this book, I would like to teach you what I consider to be emotionally and spiritually mature answers to the three spiritual questions. I hope and I pray that what you learn here will help you grow into the person God intends you to be.

1

THE FIRST SPIRITUAL QUESTION: DO YOU WANT TO GET WELL?

Our first spiritual question can be found in the story about Jesus healing a man at the pool of Bethesda found in John 5:1-9. I think that when most of us read a gospel story like this, we focus on the act of healing that takes place. That is truly miraculous. If that is all we did, however, we would miss the really meaningful and short interaction that Jesus has with a man who is an invalid. As we will see, we all have a part in an act of healing. There is nothing God can do for any of us, given our free will, if we are not willing to let him heal us.

As we should always do, let us seek to understand the context of this story.

John 5:1-9

"Some time later, Jesus went up to Jerusalem for a feast of the Jews" (v. 1). We know that in the Jewish calendar there are three main feasts. Given the timing of this story in the life of Jesus, the feast referred to here was probably Pentecost, one of the most important events in the Jewish calendar. It was customary for Jews from all over to make the pilgrimage to Jerusalem for this feast. Jesus was not from the capital city, and the verse says Jesus went there for this purpose. It would be customary for the honorable Jewish man to "hang out" in the temple or be involved in religious activities. Already at this time Jesus was considered a teacher and a rabbi, and he may have come to exercise his right to teach, although he hadn't begun yet.

"Now there is in Jerusalem near the Sheep Gate a pool, which in Aramaic is called Bethesda and which is surrounded by five covered colonnades" (v. 2). This gate was included in Nehemiah's rebuilding of the wall of Jerusalem in 445 BC. It is one of ten gates listed in Neh. 3 as part of that project. Some of the gates, like this one, were named for the activity that went through them. In this case, sheep were led into the city for the sacrifice. There is also, for example, the Fish Gate, the Horse Gate, the Water Gate, and (my personal favorite) the Dung Gate. The Dung Gate was the gate through which the garbage was taken to be burned outside the city.

In Jesus' day the pool of Bethesda was surrounded by five decorated colonnades that were like interior covered porches. The only time the name Bethesda appears in the Bible is in this verse in John. The name Bethesda means "house of mercy." The source of the pool was a nearby spring. The historian Josephus many years later described a pool that was part of the sheep market. In recent years the site of the pool has been excavated and can be visited. In our day, the name Bethesda has been used for hospitals, like Bethesda Naval Hospital, and for ministries that focus on healing and mercy.

"Here a great number of disabled people used to lie—the blind, the lame, the paralyzed" (v. 3). This pool must have had a wonderful reputation for healing, since a "great number" of really sick people came to lie there.

"For an angel went down at a certain time into the pool and stirred up the water; then whoever stepped in first, after the stirring of the water, was made well of whatever disease he had" (v. 4, NKJV). The great tradition of this pool was its healing property. At periods during the day an angel would come down and swirl or stir the waters, and the first person to get in would be healed of whatever disease he or she had. Some translations of the Bible, such as the *American Standard Version* and the King James Version, refer to what the angel did as "troubling" the water. I like this translation in some ways for what it might mean to the spiritual message of the story. "Troubled waters," with apologies to Simon and Garfunkel, have at times shown us that they can strengthen us or that we can build bridges over them.

Imagine how challenging it would have been to be the first person in the pool if you were blind, lame, or paralyzed. It was a naturally competitive situation and could have been an exercise in continual frustration for many. Some commentators have said that the healing that took place was because of the cleansing nature of the water. It was natural water from a spring, and so the reference to water here, they suggest, is only symbolic of the real healing available through God. Whether or not a heavenly angel did something mystical or sacramental to the water to give it healing qualities is not as important as realizing that God is responsible for the healing. But what is clear is that throughout the Bible water is continually used as a symbol of cleansing and healing. Not the least of this is represented in the cleansing power of water in baptism.

"One who was there had been an invalid for thirty-eight years" (v. 5). What first strikes me about this verse is how this man must have felt. He had been coming to this pool every day for thirty-eight years and hadn't been healed. Wouldn't he be feeling a great deal of despair and desperation? How envious he must have been of those who did get healed. Remember, if you had to be the first in the pool, this man would have had no chance. Yet he still came. As we continue our study of this story, think about what you would be like if every day for thirty-eight years you had gone through the same routine. Might it not be true that any of us would get so used to this routine that it would become "normal." We would know the role and how to play it. Consider also that even though we aren't told how old the man was or how old he was when he became an invalid, thirty-eight years was already longer than the normal life expectancy in those days. For this man, it was a very long time.

Then, of course, we must understand what the word "invalid" means. "Invalid" is the English word used in the *New International Version*. Does this mean the man is "not valid," that is, "not real"? Other translations, such as the King James Version, use the word "infirmity." The *New Living Translation* simply says

that this man was "sick." Have you not always thought, as I
did, that since Jesus tells him to "rise up" and to "walk," he must
have been one of the paralyzed ones mentioned elsewhere in
the gospel? Remember that Jesus spoke in Aramaic and John
wrote in a Greek. The Greek word is *astheneia* and can mean
a weakness of mind or body. The word can refer to a physical
sickness or a moral weakness. It could have been a muscle
weakness, since *astheneia* is the Greek root word of the medical condition in English called myasthenia gravis. In other New
Testament verses *astheneia* is also used to refer to a weakness
of soul (Rom. 6:19); a lack of human wisdom, skill in speaking, or leadership of men (1 Cor. 2–3); an inability to restrain
corrupt desires and a proclivity to sin (Heb. 5:2); and/or an
inability to bear trials and troubles (Rom. 8:26).

Given the general description of the crowd that gathered at
the pool, most commentators on this passage believe that "invalid" or "infirmity" here refers to a physical weakness. I accept this
interpretation, but as we will see, the truth of the question Jesus
will ask can also be applied to a weakness of mind or soul.

**"When Jesus saw him lying there and learned that he had
been in this condition for a long time, he asked him, 'Do you
want to get well?'" (v. 6).** Let's start to put some of this scene
together so we can understand how remarkable this question
is. First, the pool of Bethesda was known to have healing prop-
erties. Second, a great number of sick gathered there trying
to be the first one in the pool. Third, one of them was a man
who had been there for thirty-eight years. Fourth, he had some
kind of weakness or infirmity. Now, if you were made aware

of all of this, what would your questions have been? The first one that comes to my mind is, "How can I help?" I think I am a helpful person. But I am also a competitive person, so I also think of saying, "Let me help you and together we'll be the first one in the pool."

Perhaps you would ask the man, "How did you get this way? What happened?" In those days, in Jewish theology based on the Old Testament, there was an assumption that if a man was sick, it might be because either he or one of his recent ancestors sinned. Both Exod. 20:5 and Deut. 5:9 say that God will punish "the sin of the fathers to the third and fourth generation." So perhaps your question could be, "What sin did you or your fathers commit to be punished in this way?"

I am a pastoral counselor and some of my training was simply to be a good listener and to be compassionate. This part of me might say, "Being here like this for thirty-eight years must be hard. Tell me about it."

On the other hand, who in their right mind would ask a man who has been coming to a healing pool for thirty-eight years if he wants to be healed or to get well? What was Jesus thinking? Wouldn't the answer to that question be obvious? I believe the wisdom of Jesus is far ahead of ours. He knows our soul and mind so much better than we do. In this case, my belief is that Jesus knew that for healing to take place, the mind and soul of the man needed to be willing for it to happen. That sounds strange because why would anyone not want healing to happen? For now, hold this thought and I will return to it later.

We must also understand through our word study what Jesus meant when he asked if the man wanted to be healed, to be made whole, or to get well depending on the translation. The Greek word here is *hugiēs* (hoog-ee-ace), which can mean "healthy" or "sound in body."[3] This word can also mean, figuratively, "sound" as in "sound speech," that is, "teaching which does not deviate from the truth."[4]

When you look at the broader meaning of the word used here, it is clear that Jesus was asking the man about physical healing; and because the word can refer to having "sound speech" or to staying in line with the truth, Jesus may also have been asking about soul healing. Jesus was perhaps associating this man's mental or spiritual well-being with his physical well-being. This also speaks to the willingness factor in this passage.

"'Sir,' the invalid replied, 'I have no one to help me into the pool when the water is stirred. While I am trying to get in, someone else goes down ahead of me'" (v. 7). I don't know about you, but if Jesus were asking me a question about healing, I would give an emphatic yes. I wouldn't mince words or make any excuses. I would go for it. The tone of this answer reflects this man's frustration. He was being a victim. He had no one to help, and in the competition of the moment, someone got in his way. He was no doubt angry and discouraged.

"Then Jesus said to him, 'Get up! Pick up your mat and walk.' At once the man was cured; he picked up his mat and walked" (vv. 8-9). If the man was looking for Jesus to sympathize with him about how terrible life is, Jesus went one better.

He healed him. There are other times in the Bible when Jesus teaches that faith makes you well. There are times when people in dramatic faith come to Jesus to be healed. This time, Jesus heals and he is the One who has come to the man and this man seemingly has no faith.

With this understanding of the text, how can we apply this question to ourselves?

What Is Your Sickness?

I suspect that all of you who picked this book up are wondering about spiritual and emotional integrity. If you aren't, then why read it. I also suspect you sense a problem in your life that is blocking you from having integrity. What is that? Is it a physical malady that you are struggling with? Is it emotional wholeness that you seek? Perhaps you don't fully believe you have spiritual maturity. Remember from our word study of this story, the nature of the man's sickness was probably some kind of muscle weakness, but there was also the possibility that something was not quite whole about this man spiritually or emotionally.

In this book, I really want to address the spiritual and emotional qualities of wholeness, health, and integrity. I will leave our theological understanding of physical healing to others who are more qualified or have greater wisdom about that. I am a diabetic, and believe me, I have prayed for God to heal me. After thirty-five years of being diabetic, my prayers today are more about controlling my disease and avoiding the consequences of it. While God has not healed me in a dramatic way, he has allowed a certain amount of peace about it spiritually and emotionally. I don't fight against it as I did at one time. For quite some time, I was really angry, but now there is a general acceptance. I do believe that having spiritual and emotional peace is a huge contributor to my physical well-being. When I don't have that, I have a great deal of stress in my life, and that is definitely not good for my blood sugar.

When I was first diagnosed, a friend reminded me of Paul's wonderful teaching about our bodies in 2 Cor. 4:7-12:

> But we have this treasure in jars of clay to show that this all-surpassing power is from God and not from us. We are hard pressed on every side, but not crushed; perplexed, but not in despair; persecuted, but not abandoned; struck down, but not destroyed. We always carry around in our body the death of Jesus, so that the life of Jesus may also be revealed in our body. For we who are alive are always being given over to death for Jesus' sake, so that his life may be revealed in our mortal body. So then, death is at work in us, but life is at work in you.

Every day when I give myself insulin and check my blood sugar, I think particularly of verse 10: "We always carry around in our body the death of Jesus, so that the life of Jesus may also be revealed in our body." When my diabetic self asks the first spiritual question, "Do I want to get well?" my answer seeks to remember that if it were not for the insulin I take every day, I would die. My body and my disease reflect the death of Jesus. But if I remember that my body is only a "jar of clay" and that my spirit inside is so much more important, my answer is that I will use my disease to glorify my hope in an eternal resurrection only possible through Jesus. "Yes, Jesus, I want to be healed, healed or whole spiritually, if not physically.

● KEY QUESTIONS

- Do you suffer from a physical disease?

- Do you live every day with anxiety about your physical health?

- Are you in chronic pain?

- What is your attitude about this suffering? Are you angry with God that it has not been healed?

- If physical healing is not possible, are you willing to be well or whole regarding your feelings about this physical problem?

Perhaps you come to this book because of emotional problems such as anxiety, depression, anger management, ADHD, or manic depression. These problems can be mental health issues that some people deal with for years or their entire lives. Maybe you've been lying by the pool in some doctor's or counselor's office hoping for new answers. Drugs have been suggested and you've tried them, but they don't seem to really heal you. You've talked to many professionals, including pastors, about this, but you wind up thinking there is no one to help you. At least, there has been no one who really seems to know what he or she is doing.

You could be so used to your unhealthy feelings that they seem like a part of your life. You've always been depressed or anxious. You've always had attention issues. Despite many attempts to stop, you still get angry. Every time you try to be upbeat, peaceful, focused, or calm, some stressful situation sends you back into your feelings. It seems as though something always gets in your way. When you imagine that Jesus is asking you if you want to be well, you say, "I've tried, I just can't shake this."

Could it be problems with addiction that you seek healing for? That was my story for twenty-five years. I first remember, at age eleven, standing around a campfire at summer camp and the director asking all of us if we'd like to give up our number one sin. I had been looking at pornography for a year and knew even then that I needed to give it up. So since I didn't know the word "pornography" back then, I wrote down the name of the magazine I would steal on a piece of paper. The director said that if we were truly repentant, God would forgive us of this sin and we would never struggle with it again. I was hopeful, but I was no sooner home from the camp when the temptation came over me again and I went back to it. Have you ever struggled with pornography these days on the Internet? Maybe you're having an affair, either emotionally or sexually with someone else.

Is it drinking, smoking, or using drugs that you struggle with? You've told yourself a thousand times that you want to quit but haven't been able to. Or is it gambling or compulsive spending that addicts you? You've lost large sums of money, but nothing seems to stop you. Maybe food is the enemy. You've tried to stop overeating many times but find yourself over and over again stuffing yourself with food that isn't good for you. It might not be an addiction, but you've tried to lose weight and just can't stay with a diet or exercise program.

If it is an addiction, you might be telling yourself that you can really quit if you wanted to. Maybe you've stopped for a while and found that you can't stay stopped. Others have complained that you need to stop. If you're a smoker, even your kids have come home from school with all kinds of "helpful" information about the dangers of doing that. It could be that you've talked to a pastor, counselor, or doctor and you weren't really able to put into practice what he or she was telling you that you needed to do. You hear the question from Jesus about getting well and you say, "Yes, heal me as long as I don't have to do any of the work, because I've tried and failed."

Some of you reading this book are having relationship problems, in your marriage, in your family, with your friends. You feel lonely, misunderstood, and that no one likes you. In the evening or on weekends you find yourself without anyone to be with. You eat alone and watch way too much TV.

You've said to yourself that your spouse doesn't "get it," or doesn't meet your needs. Sex happens too often or not often enough. Money is a problem. The kids seem out of control.

Sometimes you wonder if you've married the right person. Your spouse always seems angry at you and always complains. When you hear Jesus' question, you are thinking, "Could he really heal my marriage?"

With all of the above, or at least some of it, you suffer from shame. Shame is the feeling that you are somehow defective, that you are not a worthy person. You believe that no one would like you if he or she really knew you. Your experience tells you that no one takes care of your needs. You are afraid to be honest about all of your thoughts and behaviors because you're afraid of what others would think.

Shame can be a feeling or self-perception that we grow up with. If we don't get enough love or nurture in our families, we can develop shame, telling ourselves we're just not worth it. Some people have been sexually and/or physically abused as children. They believe that somehow they caused the abuse or deserved it. These people say to themselves, "If I was a good person, these things wouldn't have happened to me." Maybe you weren't affirmed or praised. Nobody listened to you. You didn't get held or touched. You continually felt left out. Any of these dynamics can create a deep sense of shame in a person. If the feeling of shame is true for you, you might be saying, "Jesus' healing is for everyone else and not for me."

Finally, the healing you seek could be that you want to have a greater faith. You struggle with doubt or a total lack of belief. You've read the Bible and gone to church, but it just doesn't seem to make sense. You see other Christians and say to yourself, "If that is what being Christian is like, I'm not sure

I want any part of that." You believe that you've prayed and asked for help, but no divine revelation comes. So when you hear this story of Jesus, you're not sure about him at all.

⊛ KEY QUESTIONS

- Are you struggling with any of these problems?

- Have you ever talked to another person about your problems?

- Have you been frustrated that no one seemed to understand you, much less been able to help you?

- Have you given up and just decided to live with the problem?

- Would you be willing to try again?

Are You Double-Minded?

I told the story above about the first time I tried to give up pornography. I really did want to be done with it *and* I wanted God to do all of the work. I didn't want to do anything. In my mind I had a hope that God would literally transform my brain and that I would never have a lustful thought again. I really wanted to be free and was hoping God would perform a miracle.

That didn't happen. I continued to look at magazines and later videos. When I was sixteen, I went to a Fellowship of Christian Athletes camp, and when one of the professional athletes invited all of us to come forward, I went down front. I was already a Christian, but that day I said to God, "I'll agree to dedicate my life to ministry, and I have two requests. The first is that you will turn me into a professional athlete. That way in my ministry I can witness for Christ. The second request is that you will take away all of my lust." I really thought ministers were not supposed to struggle with anything, much less sexual sin, so it should be a "no brainer" for God to heal me of that. Again, he didn't do it.

The professional-athlete request was not answered either. I really thought, being a tennis player primarily, that I would go on to tennis glory and one day I would win the Wimbledon, the great English tennis tournament. The very next year I was playing in the Illinois State High School Tennis Tournament. I thought I would just "cruise" on to the championship, and then it would just be a matter of time before I was at Wimbledon. In one of the early rounds, a very short and young-looking little "kid" came out on the court to play me. I said, "I'm going to have my way with this kid." Well, this kid turned out to be a very young Jimmy Connors. He beat me handily that day, and it was he who went on to tennis glory and, yes, it was he who would go on to win Wimbledon. This was devastating to me. What later made it worse was that Jimmy Connors went on to marry a woman who had posed nude in one of the national magazines.

When I got married to my high school sweetheart, Debbie, I believed that marriage would be the answer. Paul says in 1 Cor. 7:1-2, "It is good for a man not to marry. But since there is so much immorality, each man should have his own wife." So I said to myself, "A wife is the answer, and she is supposed to fulfill her 'marital' obligations." But I skipped over mine. As I went off to the honeymoon, I was thinking that I was done with pornography. But even though our sex life was very normal and very satisfying when it happened, I still returned to pornography.

By this time I was pretty angry with God. For ten years at several major events in my life I had been praying and asking God to heal me and he didn't. I was to the point where I just thought that God must not care. In my discouragement, I continued on with lust, and my sexual addiction got worse.

Finally, in 1987 I wound up going to a treatment program for sexual addiction. While I was there, I had to work on some of my issues. I had been depressed for a long time. I was a workaholic too. My relationship and intimacy skills were awful. There were many issues to look at. One day, as I sat outside, I felt the presence of God very dramatically in my life. I felt him telling me, "Mark, I will take care of you, and you will need to learn how to care for yourself." It was Jesus' question, "Are you willing to get well?" It also meant, "Are you willing to work hard at staying sober? And are you willing to work hard on all of the emotional and spiritual problems you have suffered with for all of these years?"

When sobriety finally was achieved for a long period of time, I began to examine my life. I realized that for all of the past years I had wanted God to do all of the work; I wasn't willing or able to do any of my own work. My basic problem was that I was not willing to tell anyone about my struggle. My shame was so great that I thought if others knew me, including Debbie, they would hate me. I believed if I got honest, I would get kicked out of ministry. So silence was my way of coping with shame.

My anger also needed work. I was angry at God, myself, and Debbie. I blamed many people and all of the sinful sexual stimuli in the world for my problems. I wasn't willing to take responsibility for my own decisions. Then I realized that one of my biggest problems was my own selfishness. There was a big part of me that didn't want to give up pornography. I enjoyed it. It was exciting. Since I worked so hard and was dedicated to the ministry and my marriage, I thought I was entitled to look at a little pornography. "Who was getting hurt?" I asked myself.

Somehow, I knew that God was asking me to join him in my healing. I needed to cooperate and work, take responsibility, examine my anger, learn how to forgive, and—most of all—learn how to get honest with myself and others. Finally, one day after I had been sober for some time, I sat in a church and listened to a sermon on grace. The minister seemed, at one point, to be looking right at me when he said, "You [really meaning the whole congregation] need to repent of your inability to accept Christ's salvation. Who are you to think that you are so bad, that you are the worst person in the world, and that God doesn't love you?" It was as if Jesus was asking me, through this man, "Mark, do you want to get well? Then cooperate and accept what has been given to you. Learn to know me better. Love others as you love yourself."

What became clear to me is that for years I had a double mind. I was willing to give up pornography as long as God did all the work. Otherwise, I had grown so used to using it as a coping strategy in my life that I wasn't sure what I would do without it. It was as if pornography had become a friend. It was a companion whenever I wanted it to be. It never said no. In my anger, I often thought I deserved to look at it.

James talks about being double-minded in the first chapter of his letter:

> If any of you lacks wisdom, he should ask God, who gives generously to all without finding fault, and it will be given to him. But when he asks, he must believe and not doubt, because he who doubts is like a wave of the sea, blown and tossed by the wind. That man should not think he will receive anything from the Lord; he is a double-minded man, unstable in all he does. (Vv. 5-8)

You see, I doubted just enough whether or not I wanted to give up my addiction. I was "unstable in all" my ways. James uses the Greek word *dipsuchos* (dip-soo-khos), which literally means "two-spirited," or "double-souled." Notice that *psushos* is the root word used in the English word "psychology," which is the study of the mind. In Jesus' day, soul and mind were considered the same. So you can be double-minded or double-souled.

Isn't it true that none of us ever do anything we are 100 percent sure about? There is always some doubt, misgiving, or second thought. So when Jesus asks us if we are willing to get well, isn't it true we are never 100 percent willing? We're never completely sure.

There are many men who come to see me for counseling, and they want to get well. There is a change they want to achieve. It is truly amazing how initially zealous they can be, really fired up. Many of them are broken and humble, and they start to get honest. At this point they have a lot of energy to do whatever it takes to get well. For some of them, however, the fire burns out and the total willingness disappears. They become disappointed and discouraged. They get angry at themselves, with God, and perhaps with me. There always was a part of them that didn't want to work that hard to change. They want God, someone else, or their counselors to have all the answers.

A part of the problem is that when these men first come in, they are usually motivated by external factors. They've lost something such as money, time, or a job. They might be in legal trouble. Their wives might be threatening to leave or divorce them. The external fears wear off, however, and now they are left with their internal motivation. Now there is doubt, and double-mindedness sets in. They are tossed to and fro like the waves of the sea. This is a real emotional and spiritual battle.

My belief is that no one will get well as long as he or she tries to deny this other part of the self. If a person tries to be too perfect and can't ever admit to making mistakes, the discouragement that sets in will defeat that person every time. It's better to embrace the doubts and double-mindedness. It's better to admit there is a part of the mind that really doesn't want to be well and has become used to being sick. Some of us know how to play the role of being sick really well.

✷ KEY QUESTIONS

- Have you ever been initially enthusiastic about some-thing and later been discouraged that your enthusiasm didn't last?

- Have you ever been angry with God for not just auto-matically healing you?

- Have you ever stopped some behavior because you thought it was destructive and later realized you missed it?

- Are you familiar with doubts?

- Do you sometimes pretend to believe something that you otherwise struggle with?

Finding Willingness

"Okay," you say, "you've convinced me that I have a double mind. Now what do I do?" Good question. I think I could be "clever" and ask, "Are you willing to be willing?" That is really the case. Finding willingness is often a matter of being willing to try something new.

How big of a risk taker are you? Have you ever tried to do something different that you weren't all that sure about? Maybe you've been down on yourself because you think you don't have any courage. That could be a lie you tell yourself. Did you know that the most difficult physical task any of us will ever learn to do is to walk? You could be a skier, a skater, a dancer, a gymnast, a diver, a bungee jumper, or a great athlete, and doing those things would pale in comparison to learning how to walk. The different muscles involved in walking are many. To learn it you will have to fall down many times. There will have to be others around you encouraging you and holding your hands until you and they are ready to let go.

Do you get the idea? In order to be willing to get well, to cooperate with God's ability to heal you, to be confident, to live with your doubts and move forward, you must be a risk taker. Somewhere inside you there is an inherent risk taker. How about driving? How many of you were petrified to take that on? You sat behind the wheel and saw the other cars coming toward you or whizzing past you, and you froze. Something or someone, however, caused you to step on the gas. Walking and driving are analogies. Let me list some things I think about when it comes to a willingness to get well:

- When you have a physical pain or symptom of something wrong in your body, you will need to have the courage to go to a doctor to get diagnosed.
- When you are depressed or anxious, you will need to talk to someone, perhaps even a pastor or counselor.
- When you suffer from an addiction, you will need to admit it to yourself and others.
- When you feel shame, you will need to talk to others and get a second opinion.
- When you have marital difficulties, you will need to ask your spouse if he or she is willing to get some help.
- When you have doubts about your faith, you will need to talk to someone who has faith.

Admitting, confessing, and simply talking are often the courageous first steps in being willing to get well. Silence is the greatest enemy of willingness I know.

If you are willing to do the things listed above, then you will be ready for the second step of willingness—you will be willing to take some action. Here are several examples:

- Your doctor may ask you to take a test, get a procedure, try a drug, or change a lifestyle habit.
- A pastor or counselor may ask you to continue to come and talk about all of your feelings and past experiences.

- A recovering addict who has been sober for a long time will invite you to come to a support group, and you will need to decide to go to one even though you "hate" groups.

- A friend may tell you that you are a beloved child of God and that you are "fearfully and wonderfully made" (Ps. 139:14), and you will need to choose to believe it.

- Your spouse may be willing to get help, and now you're going to have to see a counselor and admit to your feelings, perceptions, expectations, and disappointments.

- A pastor or deeply spiritual person may ask you to study the Bible with him or her, go to church, come to a class on faith, or simply meet for coffee to talk more.

These are all basic examples. *Can you see that willingness is often a matter of asking for help?* In our story of the man at the pool, he didn't ask Jesus for help; Jesus asked him if he was willing. How about you? Are you willing to ask Jesus for help?

One of the most powerful movements in the world over the last seventy-five years has been Alcoholics Anonymous (AA). It began in 1935 by a man named Bill Wilson who had been an alcoholic and who had recently finally stopped drinking. One day on a business trip he was in a strange town and staying in a hotel. As he passed the bar in the hotel, the old temptation to drink began to overtake him. Immediately he found a phone directory of local churches and began to call the pastors. He asked if any of them had an alcoholic in their churches. Every pastor seemed surprised and dumbfounded by the question.

Finally, one of them said, "Oh yes, Dr. Bob Smith, who is one of our members, is widely known as the town drunk."

So Bill went out to Dr. Bob's house. Dr. Bob was alone and had stopped practicing medicine because of his drinking. He was afraid that Bill had come to "preach" at him about the evils of drinking and told him in no uncertain terms to "get lost." Bill was not there to preach, however. He was there because he simply wanted to talk to another drunk. He was not offering to help; he was asking for help. That night, Bill W. and Dr. Bob (as they are known by millions of recovering alcoholics) had the first meeting of AA. Before that meeting, Dr. Bob was not willing to get well. What he needed was someone to demonstrate to him how to ask for help. It was in being a friend, companion, and fellow drunk that he finally (after years of drunkenness) came to his senses and got sober.[5]

Finding willingness, as this story suggests, may simply mean finding others who can model willingness to you. Finding those people may mean asking for help.

● KEY QUESTIONS

- What kind of healing do you need? Review all possibilities.

- Do you know anyone who has needed similar healing and who has been successful in finding it?

- Have you ever been able to ask for help?

- Who are the people that specialize in providing help for the kind of problem you have?

- Would you be willing to talk to those people?

Every day in my practice I get calls and emails from people who want to get well. Sometimes those contacts are from the spouse of someone who needs to get well. That spouse is "investigating" the kind of help that is "out there." Right away I know who is the most likely to get well. You guessed it. It is the person who has asked for help and usually not the person for whom help has been sought.

And when I get that person in my office or in one of my workshops, my first question is still going to be, "Do you want to get well?" That is always the place to start. The men who come to me often say, "I wouldn't have come [sometimes from all over the world] to you and been willing to pay your fees if I didn't." Even with that response I'm going to have to see that willingness demonstrated over time. These men are asking for help, but are they now willing to do whatever it takes, whatever I tell them to do? Getting well is for the long haul, not the quick fix.

Remember also that the Greek word Jesus uses also means "whole" in both body and mind. A willingness to get well from a specific problem, like addiction in my case, will include a willingness to look at the wellness of the soul and mind. Willingness will mean a desire to get well despite all the doubts, all the work, and all the grief of giving up long-held habits. Willingness will mean trusting God even if you're not always sure God will help.

I remember early on in my healing journey that one of my friends, referring to the counselor he was seeing, said, "If he told me to go stand in the corner on my head because it would help me get well, that is what I'd do." I've never tried that with any of my clients, but I do know that the ones who are willing to ask for help humbly and then trust the guidance of others who have been successful are the ones who will get well.

A willingness to heal means having the courage to move forward, to take risks, to ask for help, to do whatever it takes, and to trust God. Only then will God meet us more than half-way.

2

THE SECOND SPIRITUAL QUESTION: WHAT ARE YOU THIRSTY FOR?
PART ONE—COPING WITH THIRST

So now you're willing, or willing to be willing. You've accepted what problems you're dealing with. You've had a conversation with yourself about your double-mindedness. In this chapter I want you to start thinking about how your problems might be related to your emotional and spiritual thirst. The second spiritual question asks exactly, "What are you thirsty for?" This question will be divided into three chapters because I want to look at what our thirst is, how we find the wrong solutions to it, what our expectations are for getting it satisfied, and what some of our perceptions of ourselves and the world might be that create the thirst in the first place.

Let's backtrack one chapter in the gospel of John to another conversation or interaction that Jesus has, this time with a woman. It is found in John 4:1-26. As we did in the previous chapter, let us look at this story in parts.

John 4:1-26

"The Pharisees heard that Jesus was gaining and baptizing more disciples than John, although in fact it was not Jesus who baptized, but his disciples. When the Lord learned of this, he left Judea and went back once more to Galilee" (vv. 1-3). As we know, the Pharisees didn't like Jesus the teacher and they were continually trying to trap him into theological controversies. In this case, it was the question of baptism, what it meant and who could do it. Jesus decided to go north to Galilee and away from Jerusalem in Judea in the south. He was emotionally tired of this debate.

"Now he had to go through Samaria. So he came to a town in Samaria called Sychar, near the plot of ground Jacob had given to his son Joseph. Jacob's well was there, and Jesus, tired as he was from the journey, sat down by the well. It was about the sixth hour" (vv. 4-6). Jesus could have decided to go around Samaria. At this time the Jews and Samaritans hated each other because of the contempt the Jews of Judea, the two southern tribes, historically had for Samaritans. The Samaritans were a group that came about because the ten northern tribes of Israel intermarried with different non-Jewish groups, starting after the Assyrians invaded their territory in 720 BC. Suffice it to say, Jewish law forbade a Jew to intermarry with a non-Jew. Even today, in conservative Jewish families if one of the children marries an outsider, he or she is immediately declared dead and a funeral service is held. So when the ten northern tribes were assimilated by a conquering people and intermarriages occurred, they were considered dead as far as the southern tribes were concerned.

So the Samaritans, one of the groups resulting from this assimilation, were despised by respectable Jews. Jesus knew he was not supposed to associate in any way with Samaritans; for Jesus to even be going through the region was a huge statement. John is showing us that Jesus breaks down old barriers and that the gospel is for everyone.

The gospel of John is always clear about Jesus' identity. He is the Son of God and the Messiah. He is "the light of the world" (8:12). In small ways John also shows us that Jesus is human. In John 4:6, he tells us that Jesus was physically tired. Jesus was a man subject to human needs. In this case he needed to rest.

The well described here still stands today. It is a well that Jacob is reported to have dug, located one-half mile south of the city of Sychar, it is ninety to one hundred feet deep. There are other wells in Sychar and to come to this well was very much out of the way. This verse tells us this well is on the land Jacob had given to his son Joseph. We all know the story of Joseph and how his brothers, jealous of his coat of many colors, had sold him into slavery in Egypt. God was good to Joseph and he becomes second only to Pharaoh in the land of Egypt and is later responsible for saving his brothers and his people during a great famine. Did you know that when Joseph died with all of his power and prestige in Egypt, he actually requested to be taken "home" and was buried by this well? (see Josh. 24:32).[6]

The Jewish twenty-four-hour day begins and ends at 6:00 AM. So when this verse tells us it was the sixth hour, we know by our clocks that it was noon. This is important to know, because people rarely went to a well in the heat of the day. Most women would go in the morning to get water for the day and in the evening to get water for the night.

"When a Samaritan woman came to draw water, Jesus said to her, 'Will you give me a drink?' (His disciples had gone into the town to buy food)" (John 4:7-8). Given the setting, time, and place, it would be very unusual for anyone to be coming to this well so far south of the city and at this time of the day. We can assume because of what we learn later about this woman (her having had five marriages and currently living with a man out of wedlock) that the respectable women of the town of Sychar probably shunned her and refused to let her draw water at respectable times or at more convenient wells. She was a woman of ill repute.

With all of this, for Jesus to even be talking to her was amazing. Think of it this way: first, she was a Samaritan, second, she was a woman, and third, she was a woman of bad character. Jewish men were not supposed to talk to any Samaritan and were never to speak to a woman in public. Jewish men weren't even supposed to talk to their daughters, mothers, or wives in public. And for Jesus to be talking to a woman of bad character, the rumors that could have started are obvious.

Here again, Jesus is breaking down a barrier. His teaching, message, and salvation are for everyone. Jesus is thirsty. He is human. He is talking to a woman he in no way should be seen with, much less talk to. This is truly remarkable.

"The Samaritan woman said to him, 'You are a Jew and I am a Samaritan woman. How can you ask me for a drink?' (For Jews do not associate with Samaritans.) Jesus answered her, 'If you knew the gift of God and who it is that asks you for a drink, you would have asked him and he would have given you living water'" (vv. 9-10). This woman knows her place and is questioning how in the world this man could be talking to her. Jesus is beginning to let her know that he is in a whole other category. He is beginning his message to her that he is the Messiah.

"'Sir,' the woman said, 'you have nothing to draw with and the well is deep. Where can you get this living water? Are you greater than our father Jacob, who gave us the well and drank from it himself, as did also his sons and his flocks and herds?'" (vv. 11-12). In a way, this woman is mocking Jesus. She is in effect saying, "Who do you think you are?" Jesus was sitting there without any way to get water of any kind. In that day, when people traveled, they usually carried a leather bucket to attach to a rope for situations just like this. Jesus sat there ill prepared. The woman must have really thought him stupid to be even talking about water.

"Jesus answered, 'Everyone who drinks this water will be thirsty again, but whoever drinks the water I give him will never thirst. Indeed, the water I give him will become in him a spring of water welling up to eternal life'" (vv. 13-14). Here we have the very essence of this story. Jesus distinguishes an amazing truth. This well, as deep as it is, contains water that seeps out of the ground. It was and is to this day not fed by a stream. It was not running or moving water. To the Jewish understanding, "living water" was a symbol of water that flows and is totally life giving.

Jesus is using a symbol that "flows" throughout the Bible. In the book of Revelation, John tells us, "To him who is thirsty I will give to drink without cost from the spring of the water of life" (21:6). In Ps. 42:2, the psalmist writes of his soul being thirsty for the living God, and later in Isa. 44:3, Isaiah tells us that God will "pour water" on those who are thirsty. Ezekiel has a vision of the river of life (Ezek. 47:1-12). The prophet Zechariah tells us that in the new world there will be a cleansing fountain and that the waters will spring forth from Jerusalem, the new Jerusalem (Zech. 14:8). *The fundamental truth Jesus is teaching is that in the human heart there is a thirst for something that only he can satisfy.*

The woman said to him, "Sir, give me this water so that I won't get thirsty and have to keep coming here to draw water." He told her, "Go, call your husband and come back." "I have no husband," she replied. Jesus said to her, "You are right when you say you have no husband. The fact is, you have had five husbands, and the man you now have is not your husband. What you have just said is quite true." "Sir," the woman said, "I can see that you are a prophet. Our fathers worshiped on this mountain, but you Jews claim that the place where we must worship is in Jerusalem." Jesus declared, "Believe me, woman, a time

is coming when you will worship the Father neither on this mountain nor in Jerusalem. You Samaritans worship what you do not know; we worship what we do know, for salvation is from the Jews. Yet a time is coming and has now come when the true worshipers will worship the Father in spirit and truth, for they are the kind of worshipers the Father seeks. God is spirit, and his worshipers must worship in spirit and in truth." The woman said, "I know that Messiah" (called Christ) "is coming. When he comes, he will explain everything to us." (John 4:15-25)

These verses reveal the deep shame of this woman because she is not married and has been divorced five times. This is an awful condition for any woman in Jesus' day. We must remember that the people of her village and the people of Samaria, although in most ways still Jewish, were also descendants of people who had intermarried with those who worshipped other gods at other places, like the nearby mountain the woman refers to. Jesus is telling her that the time will come when all people will worship God in truth. Finally, this woman reveals that she does have faith in the coming Messiah. She is, in her heart, a true Jew in her expectations.

"Then Jesus declared, 'I who speak to you am he'" (v. 26). Now, we have, in very short form, the revelation. Jesus tells her that he is the Messiah, the One who has been expected. As a Christian counselor, I am amazed at the compassion of Jesus in this story. He is talking to a person he in no way should be talking to. He is safe enough that this woman is sharing with him. It is this woman of ill repute who is one of the first to hear the gospel message from the very lips of Jesus. As a sexual sinner myself, I take great comfort in a story like this. If Jesus is offering living water to one such as this, he is showing us that his salvation is for all people, male and female, of every tribe and nation, even those with the worst kind of history.

Make of it what you will, dear reader, but this woman is the one who first goes into the village and, even with all her shame, gives her testimony of what has happened to her. Later we learn, **"Many of the Samaritans from that town believed in him because of the woman's testimony" (v. 39).**

In understanding this story, I have tried to explain the context of it so that you will have an understanding of the symbols and the meaning. If I were to summarize it, the message is clear. There are those who might try to satisfy their thirst with water that is not living. Water from Jacob's well was stagnant, not flowing. It is a symbol of stagnant ways a person might try to quench his or her thirst with anything that is not thirst quenching in the deepest spiritual sense. The truth is, only "living water" can satisfy.

The woman at the well had an obvious soul thirst. She was a shunned and shameful person. She was not satisfied in marriage and family. She was probably very lonely not being accepted by other people. Can you see how her soul was thirsty? She probably thought she was thirsty for love, respect, acceptance, friendship, or forgiveness. When Jesus asked her to call her husband, he was cutting to the chase of her problem. I imagine that when he told her the water of Jacob's well at which they were talking was not satisfying, it was a symbol of unfulfilled love and marriage. Jesus was really telling her that another relationship with a man would not satisfy her spiritual desires, her longings, her thirst.

It is important to see that this woman probably identified her longings as physical or emotional in nature. Jesus was telling her that all solutions to physical or emotional longing or thirst are spiritually based, that is, based on a relationship with him.

Our question thus is, "What are you thirsty for?" Have you ever thought a new relationship, marriage, or friendship would satisfy your thirst? Have you wondered if more exciting or frequent sex would be the answer to your sexual thirst? Do you believe that a better job or more money would bring you freedom from financial anxieties? You therefore thirst to get a different job, earn better pay, or win the lottery. You might go to casinos hoping to hit it big. I love you had something to eat when you're lonely? Maybe you have used some kind of drug, even caffeine, to help you feel better or less depressed. Perhaps you have tried other kinds of drugs, like marijuana, to bring your mood down or to relax you.

The challenge I want to address in this chapter is that most of us have tried to quench our spiritual thirst in physical and emotional ways, ways that can never satisfy. Those who drink nonliving water will always be thirsty again. This is a vital concept and hard to explain. Let me give you a couple examples.

John[7] was a very successful person in every respect. He had a thriving medical practice and a wonderful wife and kids, and he was an important leader at church. Since childhood, however, John had never felt appreciated in his family. He is the youngest of four older brothers, all of whom were quite successful in academics and athletics. It always seemed to John that they, and particularly his oldest brother, got all the praise. By the time John was born, his parents were a little "worn out" and didn't always give John as much attention as the others. So John works, makes money, and accumulates accomplishments but never feels affirmed. His wife, lately, has been telling him that he seems to be a workaholic.

Lisa has been lonely most of her life as well. She is the oldest child in her family. Both of her parents had to work to make ends meet, and as a result, Lisa over the course of her early life had to be alone and self-sufficient. Today she is married to a man who, like John above, is constantly working. When she is alone, even with the kids, she finds great "comfort" in eating. Lisa is now fifty pounds overweight, and her husband is spending less time with her emotionally, physically, and sexually.

These are just two stories of the hundreds I know in which people are seeking to satisfy their spiritual thirst by using a substance or practicing a behavior to meet that thirst. In my work, I call that coping. As the Bible tells us, we all desire a relationship with God; he is the only One who can fulfill our deepest desires of the heart. John and Lisa are coping with their unmet desires, or thirst, by working or overeating.

I want to challenge you to think about your thirst and how you might be coping with it in ways that will never satisfy that thirst.

Coping Substances

This is not a textbook on substance abuse. I'm not suggesting that the use of a substance automatically makes you an addict. What I am asking you to consider is whether or not there are times when you are physically or emotionally tired, sad, or depressed in which you ingest some substance to elevate your mood. Are there other times when you are anxious, angry, stressed, fearful, or simply can't seem to pay attention when you use some substance to calm your mood or to try and get rid of the mood altogether?

I remember discovering the wonderful mood-elevating quality of coffee during my first year of college. Those were days when I would study late into the night and then get up in the morning to take a test. All the way through seminary and graduate school coffee was my "drug of choice" to get me going. Lately my cardiologist has been telling me to cut down on my coffee drinking, so I have bargained with him and myself that drinking Diet Coke might not be as bad.

During my graduate school days I thought it might look academic, a la J. R. R. Tolkien or C. S. Lewis, to smoke a pipe. I discovered how stimulating tobacco can be. Nicotine became a favorite drug of mine.

Along the way, I knew but denied that I was gradually needing more and more of both caffeine and nicotine to achieve the same mood-elevating effect in my brain. As my heart doctor got me off caffeine, my dentist convinced me that my mouth was a "five alarm fire." So out went the pipe.

These are just two examples from my own life. Not really that dramatic and yet for years I put substances like these into my body thinking that one day I would stop and that in the meantime no harm was really being done.

By the grace of God other harder drugs were never a problem for me. Over the years, however, I have had the chance to work with many people for whom alcohol, marijuana, cocaine, and even heroin became a regular and addictive habit. In every case, I could see how these people were using the drugs to elevate or depress their mood depending on the feelings they were having at the time. More and more I could see how people were avoiding or "coping" with painful relationships and feelings inside themselves by using these drugs.

Of course, for those who become addicted to some substance, there is always hope. If a person can get the support to stop, such as in a twelve-step group or in counseling, then the brain will readjust, return to its normal state, and detoxify itself. If a person is not willing to stop an addictive pattern, then emotional, social, relational, financial, and even legal consequences can be the result.

When tempted to judge an alcoholic, drug addict, or simply a person who drinks too much coffee or smokes too many cigarettes, I remind myself that they are thirsty for something. They are in a lot of pain. The pain and the thirst often cloud judgment and make it hard to stop. It is important in the healing journey for a person to know that any drugs are a very poor substitute for the only relationship that truly satisfies thirst, a relationship with God. Alcoholics Anonymous, which has never considered itself a religious movement, says in its second step, "We came to believe that a Power greater than ourselves could restore us to sanity."[8]

Maybe it might be a doctor, friend, son or daughter, or spouse that asks you to stop using a certain substance. Perhaps those around you only see what you're doing as a nuisance and believe you will stop when you are ready. You might only be an occasional user and not really an addict. There will always be times when certain substances have meaningful uses. This is not a book to prove to anyone that he or she has a problem with a substance. The question remains the same, "What are you really thirsty for?" What are you hoping the substance will help you with, and in the long term or in the ultimate scheme of things, does it really do that?

● KEY QUESTIONS

- From the time you get up in the morning to the time you go to bed at night, what substances do you ingest into your body?

- Which ones do you use to elevate your mood?

- Which ones do you use to depress or relax your mood?

- Have you ever thought that one or more of these substances are harmful to you?

- Have you ever tried to stop but weren't able to?

- Would you be willing to stop?

Coping Behaviors

Just as substances can take your mood up or down, so can behaviors. In some cases the behaviors distract you from what you're feeling. In other cases they help you avoid your feelings. Finally, in some cases the behaviors actually stimulate chemicals in your brain that act in the same way as ingested substances do.

Distractions and Avoidance

Before we begin to understand coping behaviors, let me say that the behaviors we will be talking about are not inherently bad. You will see as we go along that most of the behaviors mentioned can be used for positive, relaxing, or recreational purposes.

I grew up in a minister's home. My father, a pastor all of his adult life, was totally enthralled with all things visual. He had grown up with an uncle who played the organ and piano for silent movies, and this love of cinema never left him. It was no wonder, then, that when the city in which we lived opened its first TV station, my dad rushed out to buy, on his salary, one of the first TV sets. From that time on, every afternoon after school and every night together as a family, the TV was on. This meant, in part, that whatever were our feelings, issues, or needs to connect, the TV distracted us from them. We were mesmerized. Ask me today any trivia question about TV from the '50s and '60s. I would like to say that I am better today, but as I write, I am also looking over my shoulder to check the score of the game being played on my fifty-inch TV.

My mother was a little different. She was not really all that interested in TV or movies. Reading and crossword puzzles were her thing. Even when she sat with us in the TV room, she was reading or doing one of those puzzles. I'm sure she was not all that happy with the constant use of the TV. Her reading and puzzling were her ways of distracting herself from the whole matter. Yet with all that she was also quick to fix us something to eat and would bring it to us on a TV tray. By the time I got to school, I knew that the real way to distract myself from the cares and concerns of my school and my friendships was by sitting in front of the TV and eating something.

We have a "border battle" in the Twin Cities, because our neighbor to the immediate east is Wisconsin. There are lots of things to compete with the "Cheese Heads" about, but none is like the rivalry between the Minnesota Vikings and the Green Bay Packers. Every Sunday in the fall there are thousands of people who either dress up to look like a Viking or a chunk of cheese. Most of this is in good fun. And for some it is an obsession. Any sports fan can use sports to help him or her relax in healthy ways, but for many sports fans it is a way they distract themselves from their otherwise boring or painful lives. This is another strategy, by the way, that my dad taught me well. As I write this, I think of all the spouses who complain about the hours their husbands or wives spend in front of the TV. You see in this way, two distractions, TV and sports, get combined.

One of the dynamics that gives my wife and I the greatest sadness when we work with couples is to see how many of them are really involved in church, but never together. Each spouse belongs separately to a men's or women's group. One sings in the choir, and the other teaches Sunday school. One serves on various boards or committees, and the other stays home to take care of the kids. The truth is, one of the spouses is usually overly involved in church. Our experience is that all of this church work is a way of distracting this spouse from the pain that exists in the marriage. Doing church work is absolutely essential to the advance of God's kingdom here on earth, but we rarely see couples doing that together.

Some of the same behaviors we use to distract ourselves we also use to avoid our feelings and desires. One behavior I see very often with men I work with is daydreaming. This is different from having positive visionary thoughts. This is different from fantasy, which we will discuss in the next section. As I'm writing this book, I'm approaching the deadline. I hate being late for anything. The thought of being late for the deadline causes me to feel fear, and I don't like fear. As I sit here by my computer, my mind is tempted to stray. There are many other things to do today. One of them has to do with planning our family's summer vacation. So I could daydream about exciting places, golfing, the beach, or whatever else we plan to see or do. To make matters worse, it's winter here, and looking out at the snow makes it very tempting to think about warmer days and places.

Another way to avoid feelings is by sleeping. One man just yesterday told me about sleeping all through the day until 4:00 PM. He was avoiding a very stressful situation at work.

Sometimes our relationships are stressful or painful. We feel angry or lonely. Rather than confront problems directly, many people choose to ignore them. I was working with a man recently who has much anxiety about money. He and his wife are spending more than they make. He, however, likes to control the finances and really never shares with his wife what the true financial situation is. She, not knowing, frequently overspends, which is her way of coping. When he brings this up to her, she says, "Well, if you made more money, then we wouldn't have a problem." Now, in addition to the anxiety about money this man feels shame and guilt. He feels he is not a good provider. He also feels angry at her for not "under-standing" and for not helping. You can see that this couple is in real trouble and a rather vicious cycle. It is all because they are avoiding the feelings created in their relationship.

I know another man who has a very difficult situation at work. His boss is very critical and demanding. He feels under-paid and underappreciated. He often has feelings of anger and resentment toward his boss and then avoids talking to him about any of it for fear of being fired. If ever his boss was to ask him how things were going, he would always say, "Oh, they're good and I'm fine."

Then there is the couple my wife and I are working with who are concerned that one of their sons is involved in drinking and immoral sexual activity. They have tried to put restrictions on his lifestyle, which the son always rebels against. Besides, they feel, he is over eighteen and so what control do they have over him? What they are avoiding is talking directly to him about their concerns. The fear is that if they do, he will just rebel even more and drift farther away from them.

In all of these situations, do you see the angers, resentments, sadness, anxieties, feelings of loneliness, and shame that are being avoided?

Now we've explored the principle that distractions and avoidance can be a way of coping with the pain of unmet needs and desires, let me simply suggest a list of some of the activities that can be used in this way:

- TV
- Reading
- Sports
- Church activity
- Work
- Hobbies
- Exercising
- Club or organization participation
- The kids' activities
- Sleeping
- Daydreaming

● KEY QUESTIONS

- Do you recognize any of these behaviors as ones you think you do too much?

- Have any loved ones in your life ever complained about a behavior you do too much?

- Has anyone ever said to you, "You're not paying attention"?

- Is there a behavior you have tried to stop but can't?

- Would you be willing to be accountable about a behavior?

- Do you ever notice that there is a behavior you do more when you are bored, lonely, angry, or anxious?

Coping Behaviors and Brain Chemistry

Certain behaviors can allow us to cope with unwanted feelings because they literally change the chemistry of the brain. This section gets a little technical, but stay with me, because it's important to understand that many of us daily try to be pharmacologists to our own brains; that is, we practice the art of self-medication.

Let's start with the woman at the well again. Jesus knew that she had been married five times and that she was living with another man. We can only imagine what her involvement was sexually with all those relationships. For the moment, consider first that this woman's life was stressful. One of the reasons she had to stay married or with a man was that single women in those days didn't fare well by themselves. Her life must have been one of survival, as well as dealing with shame and ostracism. All of these difficulties must have activated her brain's survival mechanism, which in turn affected how she felt. In short, the brain's survival mechanism produces adrenalin, which is one of the most powerful chemicals in our body. It gives us that feeling of being "high" and is thus a natural anti-depressant.

There are many activities a person can do to stimulate adrenalin. Work with all of its deadlines is one. Driving fast, taking risks, climbing mountains, bungee jumping, or playing extreme sports (such as skiing) can also do it. The main thing to remember about adrenalin is that anything that creates and sustains fear and anxiety stimulates adrenalin.

Over the years I have worked with a number of professional athletes, TV and movie stars, rock stars, and country music stars. They would all say the same thing: the natural fear of maintaining the admiration of large crowds and audiences, the thrill of fame and glory, and the literal excitement of performance are like a drug. In all cases they were referred to me because of sexual sins. It is clear to me that after a game or concert or movie is wrapped up, there is a natural "letdown" of the adrenalin needed to sustain the performance. Literally, they detox from adrenalin and will often find different kinds of stimulation to sustain the adrenalin level.

New sexual encounters, with their elements of provocativeness and excitement, will stimulate adrenalin. Even if sex is not involved in producing adrenalin, the stimulation of new relationships in general can do it. Think of how exciting whatever relationship you are in, hopefully your marriage, was when you first met. We call it "infatuation," and it is full of "happy" brain chemicals that are involved in meeting, pursuing, and falling in love. Helen Fisher, who is a brain researcher, showed a group of women pictures of the men they loved and then scanned their brains using FMRI radiology.[9] Dr. Kaplan was thus able to see the brain activity associated with an intense feeling of pleasure. That feeling of pleasure has often been compared to heroin. The technical name for the brain chemicals involved is catecholamines, but don't get too hung up on that. Just remember the feelings of love, romance, and excitement you felt when you first fell in love and you'll get it.

I don't want to be guilty of reading into our Bible passage from John 4, but what those relationships with different men were like for the woman at the well is interesting. Perhaps she did know the excitement of adrenalin and the power of love and romance. Perhaps that was the "water of the well" of which she was drinking too frequently. I am always amazed by the famous people I work with and the "normal" men who have one affair or sexual encounter after the other. In most cases they are married to beautiful, smart, talented, and loving women. In the case of the men who are famous, they might be married to women who are on the covers of magazines and whom many other men lust after. Yet they still get involved in repetitive romantic and sexual encounters because of the factors I've been describing.

And then there are the brain chemicals that are produced when we have sex. The entire sexual response cycle consists of initiation, excitement, stimulation, orgasm, and relaxation. Initiation and excitement are driven by adrenalin. This starts the pleasure center of the brain, which involves the brain chemical dopamine. I call it the James Brown drug, because when it happens we say, "I feel good." Stimulation involves touching and that produces oxytocin, which creates a feeling of well-being. Nursing mothers bond to their babies through the sense of well-being both mother and child have. All of us feel better when we get touched sexually or nonsexually. If babies are not touched enough, they have what's called a "failure to thrive" and can stop growing. Orgasm produces the same brain chemicals, catecholamines, which were described above in relation to love and romance.

When you put this all together, the front end of sex consists of a high that has been compared to cocaine. Oxytocin is somewhat like the feeling that marijuana produces. And the catecholamines are like heroin. Can you see why sex, even with a spouse, is very powerful for brain chemistry? Some of us, including me, have become addicted to this high because the brain always adjusts to what we put into it (tolerance), and we then will need more and more (escalation) to achieve the same effect. Unfortunately, even just thinking about sex or looking at pornography can do the same thing.

Now all of this is a very simplified look at the chemistry of the brain. The sophisticated reader will perhaps have some corrections or additions to what I'm saying. By the time you're finished reading this book, given the rapid advance in brain research, what I'm teaching you may have undergone further development. The important point is that sexual and romantic behaviors create very powerful brain chemicals. Some of us, not all, get addicted to them. When we engage in sex, it can be for the purpose of changing the way we feel. Many of the couples we work with complain about the boredom in their sexual relationships. Such a sentiment could be because of the tolerance effect of brain chemistry. It could also be because one or both partners are using sex, not to connect intimately, but to avoid intimacy.

In either case, more sex or more varied sexual activities are never the answer. Biologically speaking, the way God has designed the brain, sex will never be satisfying unless a husband and wife are spiritually connected. Then the powerful brain chemicals of sex are an expression of the connection of spirit, a relationship grounded in Christ, an intimate feeling. God knows that the only way such a connection will satisfy for a lifetime is if the couple is spiritually and emotionally connected.

This is a lot to digest. I learned it personally. After I got sober from sinful sex in my life twenty-five years ago, and really learned how to be intimate with my wife, sex transformed into the experience God intended it to be. I knew one Hollywood star who had sex with hundreds of women and told me, "It was never enough." I told him the story of the woman at the well and explained that one more "drink" of sex was not going to satisfy his thirst for connection. I told him his soul was thirsty for a relationship with Jesus. Although he didn't get down on his knees and accept Christ at that moment, he did later at a church service. He called me not long afterward and said, "I now know what you mean. Sex with my wife has become everything God intended it to be." To this day, he is faithful. Hallelujah!

Sex is not the only behavior that produces adrenalin or dopamine. I am not a gambling addict because I know that if I ever went to a casino or bought a lottery ticket, my brain would get a "hit" of adrenalin from the excitement. It is dangerous to spend money you may not have, and it is stimulating to think that perhaps you will. The atmosphere at casinos is usually bright with lots of noise. What a high it can be to fantasize about the wealth you are going to have when you hit it big. I am often sad when I drive by a casino and see the buses that have brought older people there. Those people spend their social security checks on feelings of excitement to distract themselves from the depression and loneliness of being old, having lost a spouse, being sick, or the fear of dying.

There are certain foods containing elements that can alter the chemistry of the brain. I do love Diet Coke. I don't know if the company that makes it put something in it that causes me to crave it. Perhaps it is just the caffeine. It's not like the early days of Coke when the name itself was a reference to the small amount of cocaine in the original formula.

I am a diabetic, so I don't eat a lot of refined sugars, such as those contained in candies and desserts. But some people need to get their sugar fix each day. Many people know that chocolate can be addicting. There are elements in chocolate, such as phenylethylamine (PEA), that have antidepressant effects in the brain. Other foods have sedative effects in them that reduce stress. There is nothing like a little nap after Thanksgiving turkey.

As I did before, let me list some of the possible ways of coping by altering your brain chemistry:

- Sex
- Love and romance
- Food
- Gambling
- Work stress and deadlines
- Activities such as sky diving, bungee jumping, or driving fast
- Any activity that you experience as new, forbidden, or dangerous
- Performance
- Attention seeking

⊛ KEY QUESTIONS (SIMILAR TO PREVIOUS ONES)

- Do you recognize any of these behaviors as ones you think you do too much?

- Have any loved ones in your life ever complained about a behavior you do too much?

- Is there a behavior you have tried to stop but can't?

- Would you be willing to be accountable about a behavior?

- Do you ever notice there is a behavior you do more when you are bored, lonely, sad, afraid, depressed, angry, or anxious?

- Are you willing to change to find living water?

In case any of you are feeling guilty or shameful at this point, let's take a gentleness break. Remember, the purpose of this chapter is to understand how many of us have sought to satisfy the thirst of our soul through false substitutes. We can cope with our thirst in unhealthy ways. We can distract ourselves, avoid our deep soul longings, or completely seek to alter the chemistry of the brain and its feelings. If you do any of this kind of coping, please know that you are not alone. Most of the coping behaviors talked about in this chapter are known to millions of people around the world. You may have learned them through the modeling of older generations in your families. Your brain might be more vulnerable to some of them.

Also, please know that you are probably coping with painful feelings that have come from past and current relationships. Most of that pain may not be your fault. You have done your best to simply get through life. Instead of beating yourself up, it would be more productive to think about getting your very real feelings healed in healthy ways. Read on. In the next chapter I want to help you understand the deep longings of your soul. You must know what you are longing for so that you can become more familiar with how to satisfy it.

3

THE SECOND SPIRITUAL QUESTION: WHAT ARE YOU THIRSTY FOR?
PART TWO—THE SEVEN DESIRES OF THE HEART

Search me, O God, and know my heart; test me and know my anxious thoughts. See if there is any offensive way in me, and lead me in the way everlasting.
—Ps. 139:23-24

In this chapter, I want to take you on a personal journey of searching your heart. At this point, you understand the words of the psalmist above. You want God to search your heart and know your thoughts, and you want to be free of offensive ways. In Ps. 37:4 we know we can "delight [ourselves] in the LORD and he will give [us] the desires of [the] heart." Jesus teaches us in Matt. 5:6, "Blessed are those who hunger and thirst for righteousness, for they will be filled."

The woman at the well was thirsty. Her heart was empty, lonely, and shameful. She was willing to be healed, as we understand in chapter 1, because she says to Jesus, "Give me this [living] water so that I won't get thirsty" (John 4:15). What are you thirsty for? Let's try to understand that.

Over the years my wife and I have experienced many seminars or workshops for couples. Most of them seek to teach couples how to communicate better, have love and respect for each other, rekindle their passion, understand life on Mars and Venus, or discover each other's love language. That is all well and good to an extent, but for some reason we have always felt there was something missing, something that wasn't quite right. Gradually, we realized that much of this instruction was about the differences between men and women. The assumption was that if we could understand how our spouses were different, we might be able to serve them in ways that would make them happy with us. Again, this is all good to a point, but one troublesome belief that could result from this approach is thinking, "If I truly understand my really different spouse, then I can change my behaviors in such a way to ensure he/she still loves me." The danger here has to do with the motivation for our service. It might be from a desire to control or manipulate rather than to serve.

We wondered if it might not be true that all men and all women are from earth. If we are all from earth, and if our faith in God's creation is true (see Gen. 1:27), then God created us male and female in his own image. At the very least both men and women have God's image in them. We have found that when we help couples understand they are both from earth and created in God's own image, it helps them be companions in the journey of the heart and not enemies from different planets.

Remember that in the Old and New Testament the heart is a metaphor for our mind and soul. So God has created in our hearts a longing for a relationship with him and with each other. So what are the desires of the heart? Over the years, Debbie and I have been developing a way of understanding those desires and believe there are seven basic ones.[10] We have written a book about those in greater detail. For this chapter, do you see that the thirst we are talking about is a soul thirst? The seven desires of the heart are ways to understand what that soul thirst is all about. Our concept is not perfect, and some of you may find other ways of understanding the heart's desires. In that case, I simply hope that this chapter helps you on your journey. The seven desires are as follows.

1. The Desire to Be Heard and Understood

Don't you like it when someone really takes time to listen to you and understand what you're saying? When someone hears and understands us, we truly feel known. Has anyone, on the other hand, ever said to you, "You're not listening" or "You don't get it?" Think about it. We like good listeners, but maybe we aren't one of them.

As you read this book, are you thirsty for someone to really listen to you? Maybe you have been trying to get something across to a spouse, a friend, a child, a relative, or a boss for a long time. Maybe you are so anxious about another person's reaction that you have given up trying to talk or you haven't even tried in the first place.

Daily, in our counseling center, my wife and I work with couples who don't feel the other person is listening. A lot of time can be spent trying to be heard. We see some people who raise their voices, even screaming. They act as if the other person is hearing impaired. We once worked with a couple in which the husband was actually deaf. The wife knew sign language, and this couple could easily communicate about most things. However, when the wife didn't feel heard, her signing would be faster and more dramatic, and often she would loudly say what she was signing.

My personal approach is simply to repeat myself until I feel that Debbie "gets it." I have trouble letting go of a conversation because there is always one more argument, rational explanation, or historical story that proves my point. Needless to say, in our early days Debbie became thoroughly afraid of my "long-windedness."

Some people revert to what they did as a child to be heard—they have a temper tantrum. This usually involves some dramatic behavior like shouting, throwing things, punching walls, and (for a few) physical violence. One of my favorite approaches was that told to us by one wife. She said that when she didn't feel heard and was totally frustrated, she would storm out of the house, get in her car, and squeal the tires as she backed out of the driveway. It did get her husband's attention.

As you reflect on this desire, and each desire whose descriptions are coming up, I want you to think about what experiences you have had with it. In this case, consider your experiences with being heard and understood. Who were the good listeners in your life? Who were not so good? How well did your parents do? Did they take time to listen to you? The other day, I was so proud of our daughter. One of her children was having a tantrum. Patiently, she knelt down, looked him in the eyes, and said, "What do you want me to know?" Amazingly, he calmed down and told her. Some of us never had that. Some of us have given up trying to be heard. We gave it up years ago. "What's the use?" we think.

Finally, with every desire, I want you to think how good you are at it. Are you a good listener or do you even know what I'm talking about? Perhaps you are not the most patient person in the world. Maybe you are busy and don't have time. Whatever is the case, start thinking about this as it relates to your understanding of the last spiritual question (see chap. 5).

● KEY QUESTIONS

- Who is the most significant person in your life? A spouse? A child? A parent? A friend?

- How is this person at listening?

- What is it that you would like this person to know? Take a minute and see if you can write down in one sentence something you would like that person to understand.

- Who were the good and bad listeners in your child-hood? Is there something that one of your parents never completely understood about you?

- When you don't feel heard, what do you do to be heard?

- Who do you feel you could listen to better?

2. The Desire to Be Affirmed

Doesn't it feel good when someone tells you that you've done a good job? Don't you love it if someone honestly thanks you for something you've done? Affirmation comes and lifts our spirit. It can energize us and really get us going. We know we are appreciated.

One of my cousins in Germany took as a foster child into her home a young girl who was a prodigy at the piano. My cousin was well-off financially and had a large house and many grand pianos in several rooms. She paid for this girl to get piano lessons with the finest teachers in Europe, and today this girl, now a young woman, is rather well-known. On a recent visit, my cousin mentioned to me that this girl has never told her thank you. It breaks your heart. Gisela didn't take the girl in so that she would be thanked. She did it out of the good-ness of her heart, but it would still feel nice to be affirmed.

How did you do growing up? Were there affirming people in your life? My belief is that the affirming people in your life are those you admire and respect the most. On the other hand, were there people in your life for whom you could never do anything right? Don't just think about your family. My fourth grade teacher was very critical of almost everything the boys in our class did. In those days good handwriting, a trait I lacked, was considered a sign of being smart. During the year she called me "Mark P," and the "P" stood for poor handwriting. To this day, I have difficulty writing on blackboards, white boards, and flip charts. Hurrah for PowerPoint!

I believe that most parents and people do the best they can. Sometimes their own hurts and life experiences make it hard for them to be affirming. Often they are very critical of themselves and, in turn, critical of others. Did you grow up thinking you could never get anything right? If you are like that, you might also be very critical of yourself. Are you also critical of others?

Be careful, too, of affirmations you may have received because they came with expectations. The expectation might simply have been that the affirmer wanted you to do some task or job again. You'll know this was your experience if today when someone gives you a compliment, you say, "Yes, but . . ." It's as if you don't want the compliment.

Ray, for example, was the oldest boy in the family. His father was a farmer and expected Ray to work on the farm when he grew up. Ray was good at music and really wanted to go to college and major in it. As he grew up, and particularly as he approached the end of high school, Ray found that his dad never seemed to have time to come to any of the concerts or performances, claiming he was too busy on the farm. Whenever Ray helped on the farm, his dad always thanked him and praised whatever he did despite Ray's perception that he had done it poorly. Ray did wind up taking over the farm, and every time someone affirms how well he is doing, he just hates it.

For those who are thirsty for affirmation, what can be done? First, ask yourself if you have ever done something you didn't want to do because you thought it might please someone else. Have you ever said yes when you really meant no because you wanted someone else's approval. Have you worked and worked and hoped that you would get your boss's approval, not to mention a raise (a form of approval).

You see that affirmation and approval are very similar. Some of you might think, or worry, that if others don't approve of you, they will leave you. In these situations, people are known to do whatever it takes to please the other person they are afraid of losing. In the meantime, those people get exhausted and sometimes resentful if they don't get the affirmation they so desperately seek.

Beware of the "but." One man I was talking to recently was raised by his grandparents because his parents had been killed in a car accident. Grandpa provided and saw to it that the man got through college, but he was also very gruff and critical. This man, today a very successful businessman, told me between sobs that one of his most vivid memories was when he got his first hit in Little League. After the game, Grandpa said, "That was a good hit, *but* you could have run faster to third base." That's giving an affirmation one moment and taking it away the next.

Some of us are affirmation challenged. We have a hard time giving affirmations. One woman's mother told her to be careful with her affirmations, because she wouldn't want others to think too highly of themselves. That might be true for some people, but it wasn't true for the woman's husband, who was desperate for a kind word from his wife.

The Bible is clear about affirmation. The Greek word translated in the NIV as "encouragement" means "to build each other up" or "to edify each other." Paul tells us, "May our Lord Jesus Christ himself and God our Father, who loved us and by his grace gave us eternal encouragement and good hope, encourage your hearts and strengthen you in every good deed and word" (2 Thess. 2:16-17). Paul also says, "Therefore encourage one another and build each other up, just as in fact you are doing" (1 Thess. 5:11).

✱ KEY QUESTIONS

- Who were the affirming people in your life?

- Who were the critical people in your life?

- Over the years what have been your strategies to get affirmations?

• When is the last time you affirmed someone?

3. The Desire to Be Blessed

Affirmations are what we hear when we've done something right. They are about our behaviors. Blessings, on the other hand, are about being praised for who we are as people. Affirmations are for what we do. Blessings are for who we are.

Think back. In your life were there people who just seemed genuinely glad you were alive. You didn't have to do anything. You were celebrated. One way to think about this is to remember, or be aware of, what stories are told about you. My dad, every birthday, would tell me, "I remember the day you were born and how thrilled I was to have a son." I hadn't done anything yet. I was celebrated. Are you celebrated? How was your birthday, graduation, or wedding handled in your family?

On the other hand, some of us get the "anti-blessing." One physician remembered that his mother, who was forty-four at the time of his birth, told him all the time, "I regret the day you were born. I had a lot of freedom until you came along." That is a painful story and very obvious. Sometimes the message is not so dramatic or obvious. One man remembers that his mom said about report cards, "I always got A's." That was it and the message was just as clear: "You're not a good or smart person." One man remembered his sister's toast at his wedding when she said to his new bride, "I never thought that anyone could love my brother. Are you sure you want to do this?"

A blessing comes with the feeling that others are proud of us, that they love us unconditionally, and that we can make mistakes and they will still be around. When Jesus was baptized, God spoke to him and said, "You are my Son, whom I love; with you I am well pleased" (Luke 3:22). In this passage, through the descent of the Holy Spirit, God's voice is telling us that this Son is the Anointed One, the One sent to save us.

Just as with affirmation, a blessing sometimes comes to us from another person because we are a good reflection on him or her. That kind of blessing often carries with it the feeling that the words are more about the other person than they are about us. One man's father used to tell him that he was proud of him and that God had a very special plan for the man's life, going into ministry. It felt good and might be right, but as the man heard it again and again, he felt it was more about glorifying his earthly father and not his heavenly Father. When this is the case, we might not really feel that the blessing is genuine or freely given.

So what do we do when we thirst for a blessing? I believe the most basic belief that some of us have is that the way to get a blessing is to do something. We don't know an unconditional blessing; in our experience everything has a condition. So we confuse blessing with our thirst for affirmation and think that the real way to get a blessing is to accomplish something. Do you ever have a conversation inside your head in which you ask yourself, "What I just did, would Mom or Dad be proud of me or pleased with me?" I know countless men who have worked themselves to death and never even received the attention of their fathers.

One man said his father never came to any of his games. Another told me his mother paid great attention to his older brother and virtually none to him. All their lives, both men struggled to get just a little recognition. They competed in sports and in business. They have wonderful families. One of these men said that ever since he entered adulthood, neither of his parents has ever visited. So he continues to work and work and work.

I struggle with the lack of my mom's blessing. I believed that when I got married, Debbie would be the solution to that problem. Because I didn't know how to be loved unconditionally by a woman, I didn't recognize her unfailing love until I messed up everything and discovered she was still willing to stay with me. That didn't mean she wasn't angry and hurt. But her love was deep, firm, and committed. Until then I thought every time she disagreed with me, said no to sex, or hurt me with her words that she didn't love me just for who I am. That was never true, but it took me a while to realize it, because my wounds from childhood were so great.

Have you ever sought a blessing by seeking to have a lot of friends? Do you try to impress people with your charm, your intelligence, your money, your house, or your car? Do you incessantly talk about yourself to build yourself up? Do you direct every conversation back to being about you? If you do, you are practicing what we technically call narcissism, which I've always thought was a "blessing disorder." People who are so self-centered are really wounded people trying to find a blessing.

How are you at unconditional love? Today, I try to let my wife know about my love for her. Even though my children are grown and gone, I still call or email and let them know how proud I am of them. This is not for what they've done, but for who they are. All three of my kids have not always done things the way I would have liked. They have made mistakes. My two sons are a lot like their father. With all of that, there is nothing they could ever do that would prevent me from loving them.

⊛ KEY QUESTIONS

- Do you still long for the blessing of your mother or father?

- What have you done in your life to try to earn it?

- Are you tired and discouraged that there is nothing you could ever do to be blessed?

- How do you try and impress people around you?

- How secure are you around your spouse?

- Do you ever go out of your way to show someone you love that you do love him or her?

4. The Desire to Be Safe

The desire to be safe is the desire we have to be free of all fears and anxieties. The first time we experience anxiety and fear is when we are born. We leave the protection of the womb, a warm and nurturing place, and come out into the "cold, cruel world." We are afraid of being dropped. Then there are these strange hands. Where did our mothers go anyway? So what do we do? We cry a lot to see if we can get the kind of holding and soothing that will help us feel safe.

From those early moments our human nature can remain anxious. It is natural because it is virtually our survival self. God put fear and anxiety in our brains to warn us of danger. When we sense real danger, we can try to avoid it and run (flight) or we can confront it head on (fight). The survival or stress response is really about avoiding injury and death. Today most of us live in a world where there are not the same kinds of day-to-day physical dangers our ancestors experienced. Still at some level we all want to be safe. We all want to live long and productive lives. We can be anxious about our health, securing food and shelter, and having enough money to live that long and productive life in a comfortable way. Also in our human spirit, we know being with someone is safer, and so we can get anxious about being alone, just like when we were born.

What I've just listed are large anxieties. How was anxiety handled in your family or upbringing? Did you feel safe? Were you provided for? Were people trustworthy about always being there for you? Or were you neglected? Were you physically abused in some way? Did certain people just seem to not care? One woman told me that her mom would always threaten to leave if she didn't correct her behavior.

It is really hard to have thoughts about death, illness, poverty, or aloneness because they can be overwhelming. It is easier to worry about smaller fears because we believe we can control them. Think about it. Do you worry about some issues that are really not "that big a deal"? I have been obsessed for years with the outside maintenance of our house, like cutting the grass; it really should be a certain height. In the fall I worry about all of those leaf "invaders," and in the winter I really do need to get all that Minnesota snow off the driveway. When all of these things are done, everything is "right with the world."

I know some people who worry just as much about the inside of the house. Do you obsess about cleanliness or the laundry? I know one woman who spends time every day combing the fringe on her oriental rugs so that it goes in the same direction. Do you ever need to line things up, put them in order, or double- and triple-check whether you locked the doors and shut off the lights? Do you like to have the checkbook balanced to the penny or have a budget you never stray from? Do you need to control *something* when many other areas of your life just feel out of control? Do you ever get mad at someone else who just doesn't seem to worry about these things as much as you do? Do others ever bug you by saying things like, "Why do you worry about that so much? It is not a big deal." Frustrating, isn't it?

When our anxieties control us, we rarely say what we really feel. Our radar is out continually for what someone's reaction is going to be, and we are always anticipating what we need to say or do to have the safest effect. Have you ever smiled in response to something you found disagreeable because you worried about what would happen if you disapproved? If someone has asked you, "What would you like to do?" was your response, "I don't care. What would you like to do?" Have you ever said to yourself, "Why did I do that? I'm such a coward"?

In any relationship our desire to be safe may override our desire to serve and love. Our survival self is very powerful. We figure out ways to manage our anxiety, control smaller things, and even direct health issues, money, and people. Our rational brain knows better most of the time. By the time this part of our brain catches up, we may be frustrated by our own anxiety. We can get anxious about being anxious.

God put the deep desire to be safe in our heart because he wants to teach us to rely on him. Psalm 55:22 says, "Cast your cares on the LORD and he will sustain you." He wants us to know that he is the One who will keep us safe. Jesus says in Matt. 6:27, "Who of you by worrying can add a single hour to his life?" God is trying to teach us to trust him and his promises.

⊛ KEY QUESTIONS

- Think about the ways you seek to create safety for yourself and for others.

- How are you at trusting others?

- How safe did you feel growing up?

- Do you ask for help or ask for what you need to feel safe?

- What do you seek to control when other areas of your life are out of control?

5. The Desire to Be Touched

The desire to be touched has two forms of expression. First, we all have a desire to be sexually touched. That is a part of our human nature, and God put it there so that we would be fruitful and multiply. Second, we all have a desire to be touched in nonsexual ways. A problem arises when these two desires get confused.

The desire for sexual touch is the energy inside of us to be productive, passionate, and creative. It is a life force that leads us to reproduce the race, build things, and invent new solutions to life's problems. The energy of this drive is much larger than just the act of sexual intercourse. It is the source of our passion and all things creative in us. The sex drive is not evil. It can be expressed in sinful ways when we don't follow God's design for healthy sexuality. This desire to be sexually touched can be sought from any person of the opposite sex, particularly those we perceive to be in the childbearing and child-rearing years. This is an instinctual drive, and as a pure biological force it knows no boundaries.

God tells us to express this biological drive only within a spiritual and emotional covenant called marriage. When that relationship is spiritually and emotionally connected, then physical passion takes on a whole new dimension—it becomes an expression of spiritual and emotional intimacy, not just a passion to be satisfied for purely physical release. This also means that we all should use the creative, productive, and passionate energy in ourselves to serve others and God. When we do that, we are pursuing our calling. When we are in tune with that, all the life force inside us is used for good.

The second form of expression the desire to be touched has is the desire for nonsexual touch. We believe that we all have a desire to be touched skin to skin and that this kind of touch doesn't lead to sex. I mentioned oxytocin earlier, the brain chemical created when we are touched. I believe we never outgrow the need for touch. Although we may be fully grown, we still need nonsexual touch. The sense of well-being that touch gives us is critical to our welfare. Yet how many of you receive nonsexual touch regularly? Oh, you say, "That's no longer necessary." Maybe you're a man and are rather uncomfortable with touch from men, or you're a woman and are also uncomfortable with touch from men. Then there's the possibility that you are just uncomfortable with touch in general.

Many of us give up on healthy, nonsexual touch. Maybe we didn't get it when we were small. Maybe we were touched in unhealthy ways, so that now we are afraid of it. Maybe it just doesn't feel comfortable. Maybe we just don't know how good it feels. So if we have given up or avoided it, we are left only with the other touch, sexual touch. This association may even start early in the life of a person. If he or she is not getting touched, he or she may learn that touching feels good, particularly in the genital area. This early discovery may lead to a pattern of masturbation later on. We might be confused and think the only way we can get touched is sexually. Those of us who have had this confusion may be really demanding about sex and, through our aggression, turn our spouses completely off.

My wife and I had to get more intentional about touch. We went through a time when I had to expressly state to Debbie that I wanted to touch her in a way that was completely nonsexual. Gradually, we came to distinguish the two kinds of touch and trust each other in our initiation of either kind. As Debbie was able to trust, she realized she didn't have to be on the defensive all the time. Enjoying nonsexual touch also allowed us to more mutually enjoy sexual touch.

Jesus demonstrated the healing power of touch. In Matt. 8:3, for example, Jesus reached out and touched a man with leprosy, and the man was healed. Lepers were not to be touched. They were considered "unclean." How many of you because of your perception of yourself, feel that you are somehow "unclean"? You have a history of sin or abuse and you don't feel worthy of God's love. God is, in truth, willing to touch you. In Matt. 9:20-22, Jesus is touched by a woman who has had a flow of blood for twelve years. Simply touching the hem of Jesus' garment is enough to heal her. When we seek to touch God and he seeks to touch us, it can be wonderfully healing. When we touch each other in healthy ways, and when a husband and wife touch each other in nonsexual ways, it can be a wonderful experience of God's healing love.

● KEY QUESTIONS

- When you were growing up, what was your experience of touch in your family?

- Did anyone, a family member, a friend, an older girl or boy, or an adult, touch you in ways that felt sexual and unsafe?

- Who touches you today?

- Who do you seek to touch in a caring and comforting way?

- What do you do when touch does not feel "right"?

- If you're married, how are you and your spouse at distinguishing sexual from nonsexual touch?

6. The Desire to Be Chosen

The desire to be chosen is the soul thirst we have for someone to select us to be in a special relationship. It starts when we are small and our parents let us know they are so glad we were born. They chose us to be their child. Then when we are not much bigger, there are children who choose us to be their friend. In school, we long to be chosen for the team (and not last) or to be asked to sit at a certain lunch table. A teacher chooses us to be in some special position for the day, week, or year. Later we yearn to be chosen for a date, maybe the prom. In our adult years we love it when we are picked to be in a club or organization or we are chosen for a significant job. Ultimately, we all long to be chosen by one other person to be in a marriage covenant. This desire for marriage also means we want to be the only one chosen. As one of the old marriage vows says, *"Forsaking all others,* do you take [choose] this woman [or man] to be your lawfully wedded wife [or husband]?"

It is a wonderful experience to be chosen. You feel special and accepted. You feel desired. We've often said that the desire to be chosen is the desire to be desired. In marriage it is the desire to be passionately desired. When you feel chosen, you create messages about yourself that are congruent with God's truth about who you are: "I am beautiful," "I am special," and "I am beloved." When you are not chosen, you create distorted beliefs about yourself that are not consistent with who God has created you to be: "I am not enough," "I am not lovable," and "I fall short of others." You desire to be chosen for who you are, and yet you sometimes go to great lengths to be things you are not in order to be chosen.

Over the course of your life, what have you done to be chosen? Have you said a yes you didn't mean to be chosen? Are there cosmetic things you've done to change the way you look? Think about our cultural fascination with looking young. Now, according to the ads, we need to have cosmetic dentistry to have a good smile. Plastic surgery is the fastest growing medical specialty. It's as if doctors and dentists can create the "ugly duckling" experience: a person was once ugly but is now beautiful. That is, he or she is now choosable.

The way we look also dictates what is choosable to wear. Do you have any experiences going out in public and just knowing you were wearing something "wrong"? How many times have you asked a friend or family member what he or she is planning to wear? How much of our advertising industry is based on how we (or our houses) look and smell? Ads claim that if we wear or use a certain product, we will be acceptable. In some areas of the country even the cars we drive are fashion statements. Part of me often wonders if I would be more choosable by driving a more upscale car, such as a BMW.

Having money contributes to how safe we feel, as we discussed above, but it can also indicate how chosen we feel. Have you ever thought, "That person is so rich," and regarded how special he or she was? Wealth, in most cultures, is a sign of desirability. So are certain types of status. Being a white-collar worker is better than being a blue-collar worker, or is it? Being the president of a company certainly means you are really smart, or does it? Working outside the home is more valued than working inside the home, at least that's the view of the world. Think about the messages you were taught growing up about what amount of money, power, or status is the most chosen.

Sadly, many cultures pick out some people to be "undesirable" or "outcasts." We start doing it in school. So and so is a "nerd" or a "geek" or a "loser." In my school days, outcasts had "cooties." It was just not good to be around them. It was as if, like leprosy in biblical days, their nerdiness would rub off on us. Were any of you born into a "good" family as opposed to a "bad" one? Maybe you were born on the "wrong side of the tracks." Painfully, some of you were born into ethnic or racial groups that culture decides are not as choosable. We will know them by the degrading names we call them.

How are you at letting people you've chosen know you choose them? Does your spouse know that? That is one of the powers of anniversaries. They are celebrations of "I would choose you all over again."

Let us remember that in our story of the woman at the well, Jesus is really breaking down uncleanness. This is a woman, a Samaritan, and an immoral woman. This is the person, in that whole area, that Jesus *chooses* to talk to. She was thirsty for being chosen, and in her willingness to understand she received the living water of Jesus' love for her. In your desire for being chosen, where are you with understanding how much

God does in fact choose you? James puts it this way, "Has not God chosen those who are poor in the eyes of the world to be rich in faith and to inherit the kingdom he promised those who love him?" (2:5).

⊛ KEY QUESTIONS

- What are the stories from your life in which you felt that you were chosen? Not chosen? Rejected?
- If you are married, how are you at letting your spouse know that he or she is still the only one and, thus, really chosen?
- In your family did you ever feel that one of your brothers or sisters was chosen more than you?
- Do you know that God chooses you?

7. The Desire to Be Included

The desire to be included is related to the desire to be chosen. This desire is broader. We desire to be included in fellowship with God and with others. We long to belong. This desire is about community. We long to be a part of something larger than ourselves. It helps us feel that we are not alone and gives us a sense of well-being. This sense of belonging gives us a feeling of needed security. Belonging has all kinds of emotional, physical, and spiritual benefits.

It is a sad thing when we don't feel that we belong even in our own family. Maybe we feel like the outcast of our family, the black sheep. Some of the people I work with were orphaned or given up for adoption. Hopefully, they were *chosen* to be *included* in a loving family. While they feel included at one level, their souls often desire to know where they came from and who they really belong to.

As we grow up, we long to belong to a group of friends. It may be the kids in our neighborhood or school. It may even be the "in" group. Others might not feel included in our "in" group, but we act as if we don't care because we're in. We belong to lots of things as children—scouts, youth groups, clubs, and teams. We all long to be included in something that helps us feel part of something larger. This desire is even behind the rise in our culture of gangs. Even though young people may be afraid of them and know they do destructive things, being in a gang gives them the feeling that they belong and that they always have somebody to "hang" with. Some gang members would even say that in some neighborhoods, being in a gang is a matter of survival.

Ask yourself how many groups you belong to or long to belong to. Consider your neighborhood and/or town. There are clubs, organizations, fraternities and sororities, and churches. Have you ever longed to be part of a group that you didn't get in? What did that feel like? What have you ever done to get into the right group? Remember that this book is all about having integrity. Have you ever said you believed something that you did not? Have you ever pretended to be something that you are not? Have you ever excluded someone from something because you wanted the security of knowing you were "right" and he or she was "wrong"?

God includes us in fellowship with himself and with his Son, Jesus, through the fellowship of the Holy Spirit. Jesus said,

"Whoever does the will of my Father in heaven is my brother and sister and mother" (Matt. 12:50). He also said, "Where two or three come together in my name, there am I with them" (18:20). Jesus tells us to include and welcome each other: "Whoever welcomes one of these little children in my name welcomes me; and whoever welcomes me does not welcome me but the one who sent me" (Mark 9:37). The apostle Paul tells us that we all have different talents and gifts but that we are part of the same body and that we belong to each other (see Rom. 12:5).

In the fellowship of marriage we include each other in all aspects of life together. When we include each other, we share feelings, thoughts, decisions, and vision together. That is a one-flesh union. In Eph. 5, Paul reminds us that this one-flesh union is like the relationship of Christ to the church. Christ includes all of the church—that is us—in his kingdom and serves us by dying for us. We believe, then, that in marriage the very image of one-flesh union says that we are connected to, include, and serve each other. When we include each other in marriage, it is more than just sharing a house, children, or a paycheck. It is honestly sharing our spirits and minds, as well as our bodies.

✱ KEY QUESTIONS

- What are all the groups, including churches, you have ever belonged to?

- When was the last time you felt left out?

- Were you ever in the "in" or the "out" group?

- What things have you done to fit in and belong?

- Would leaving a certain group give you a sense of anxiety?

- Where do you feel included today?

Finally, consider a belief of mine about fantasy.[11] I believe that every fantasy a person can have is an attempt to get one or more of the seven desires met. You might have sports fantasies in which you "win the big game" and get lots of affirmation, which you might even think is a blessing. If you fantasize about winning the lottery, having lots of money in your mind might be your attempt to feel safe. Sex, love, and romance fantasies, and remember the brain chemistry they can produce, will usually have people in them who are good at listening, affirming, loving unconditionally, being safe, touching a lot, choosing only you, and including you. Do you get the idea?

Fantasies are those creations of our imagination that might be based on past events or hoped-for future ones. This is a short summary of a very important principle. For now, ask yourself these questions:

1. Do you recognize that you have fantasies?

2. Can you be honest with yourself about what they're about?

3. Consider your desires, and see if you can see a connection between the fantasy and one or more of the desires.

Fantasies are very different from honest dreams and vision. Vision about your life creates mental pictures of your calling from God. Fantasies are your attempt to heal the wound of neglected thirst. Fantasies are about thirst. How many fantasies have you had? Have they ever satisfied anything?

Take some time to digest all the material and questions from this chapter. It will help you identify two things:

1. The deep desires and thirst of your heart

2. How you may have coped in unhealthy ways with some or all of them, including any fantasies

In preparation for the next chapter, let me suggest you review the chapter on your willingness to be healed (chap. 1). In order to have integrity, we will be talking more about a willingness to be healed of the unhealthy ways we try to get our thirst quenched from the wrong well.

4
THE SECOND SPIRITUAL QUESTION: WHAT ARE YOU THIRSTY FOR?
PART THREE—PUTTING IT ALL TOGETHER

Now that you understand all the desires and have worked on the key questions, it is time to put all of this together as it relates to your thirst. In this chapter I want to lead you through some exercises or assignments that will help you know your thirst, your false substitutes for that thirst, and what living water is all about. This chapter is slightly different because it will be short and contain suggestions for your meditation and journaling and for your conversations.

Assignment One

Think back over your life and all the different people in it. Make a list of the most important ones, such as parents, teachers, siblings, friends, pastors, and spouse. Leave room beside each name, and for each one ask yourself if you experienced being heard and understood, affirmed, blessed, safe, touched in healthy ways, chosen, or included by that person. Write your answers next to the names. Don't be afraid to be honest, and don't worry about being a complainer or victim. This exercise is not about judging anyone. It seeks to root out any feelings of loss, anger, and resentment you may have.

Assignment Two

Now list all of the seven desires, and again leave yourself enough room by each. For each one that you felt you didn't quite get growing up, make a list of all the different ways you might have coped. Go back to review the last two chapters, including the lists on unhealthy thirst quenching that were written about in chapter 2. Be as honest as you can and be courageous. Remember that you are striving for a life of integrity. Also list any fantasies that you might have had.

Assignment Three

Again, looking at the seven desires, consider and list all of the unhealthy beliefs and attitudes you have developed in your life because you did not get some of the desires met. Here is an example:

- If I was a lovable person, I would have been chosen.
- I would have been affirmed if I could get anything right.
- No one really wants to be with a person like me.
- If I could explain myself more, someone would listen.
- My dad really loved me; he was just never able to express it.

- I deserved to get hit because of my bad behaviors.

In order to get at this list, you may want to ask a friend or your spouse if he or she would be willing to listen to some of the stories from your past. Ask God to help you remember any stories for which you need healing. Tell your friend or spouse how these stories make you feel about yourself, the world, others, God, and life.

Assignment Four

Ask yourself if you have expected others in your present life to meet the seven desires. Consider that you might have created some symbols for the desires. For example, when you get that promotion, you interpret it as a blessing. When you accumulate a certain sum of money, you feel safe. When your spouse says yes to sex, you feel chosen. List all the people whom you have had expectations of and then write what those expectations are next to each person's name.

Assignment Five

Now consider what is really true about you and about your relationship with God. Again, list the seven desires and ask yourself if all those core beliefs about yourself that you developed throughout your life are really true. Does God think about you in the same way you think about yourself? Would it not be true that you are fearfully and wonderfully made and that God has forgiven all your sins? Next to each desire, write down ways you think God has met or can meet that desire. Is God a good listener? Does he affirm? Has he not chosen you and included you in his kingdom. Think of times in your life when you really did feel the presence of God. If you can't think of any, would you be willing to talk about this with a pastor or a person you consider a spiritual person?

Assignment Six

Are you willing to stop all the ways you have sought to quench your heart's desires, your thirst, in unhealthy ways? If you haven't already, would you be willing to read the first book in this series on accountability?

Assignment Seven

This assignment is really preparing you for the last chapter and the third spiritual question. This time make a list of all the people in your life today that you really love, such as your spouse, children, other family members, and friends. Next to their names write down how you do at serving their seven desires. Do you listen, affirm, bless, keep safe, touch in healthy ways, choose, and include them in your life?

This is a lot of tough work. If you have even just thought about the assignments without any journaling, writing, or talking about them, congratulations! It takes courage to do this work. If you just can't bring yourself to consider these things, fine. Move on to the next chapter. You may find motivation there that will allow you to return to these assignments. Finally, if you feel many emotions are surfacing for you while doing this work, stop for a while and talk to someone you trust. The bottom line is that if you are affected in this way, don't let yourself be alone and don't turn to any of those wells that don't satisfy thirst.

5

THE THIRD SPIRITUAL QUESTION: ARE YOU WILLING TO DIE TO YOURSELF?

We come to our last spiritual question: "Are you willing to die to yourself?" It is last because it is the hardest to answer and the one that will reach into the deepest part of your soul. You can't even come to this question without answering the first two questions: "Are you willing to be well or whole?" and "What are you thirsty for?" You see, you must be willing to deal with how tough this last question is, and you will need to distinguish what you're really thirsty for from any false substitutes. Answering yes to this question means that you are willing to give up your unhealthy attempts to quench your thirst and discover what really matters.

In this chapter we will continue our study of the interactions Jesus has with people in the gospel of John. This time we will look at Jesus' conversation with Mary and Martha in John 11:1-

43. It is one of the most dramatic stories in the New Testament. It is the story of Lazarus. Before we get to that powerful story, I want to ask one more preliminary question: "What are you willing to die for?"

If you are going to confront the question about dying to yourself, you will need to consider what part of your life might be selfish. Any person who wants to change his or her life in order to live a life of greater integrity will need to live a life that is the opposite of selfishness. Would you not agree that the opposite of selfishness is selflessness? For years I have been seeking to help men understand selflessness as opposed to selfishness.

I work with men who are addicts. Their addictions are selfish ways of trying to quench the deep-seated thirst that is in the soul for all of the desires I wrote about in chapter 3. Addicts are selfish and they are in a lot of pain. This is not just the pain resulting from their addictive behaviors. It is the pain that comes from unhealthy relationships in the past and in the present. Addicts are generally people who experienced a great deal of pain growing up. They usually didn't have healthy relationships with their parents and with others. Some parents for a variety of reasons may be neglectful, just not present for their children's needs. We call this a form of abandonment.

Addicts have shameful core beliefs about themselves that they are bad and worthless and that no one will love them as they truly are. They have core beliefs, based on their life experiences, that no one will meet their needs and desires. As a result of these beliefs and experiences in life, addicts will tend to form unhealthy relationships in the present. They don't know how to love in healthy ways. They lie about themselves because they think that if others knew the truth about them, they would leave them. The pain addicts experience in the past is therefore repeated and perpetuated in the present.

Addicts carry a great deal of anger and resentment about not getting their needs met. They are sad about their losses. It is the pain of sadness and the pain of anger that drives them to selfishly seek to get their needs and desires met. They just don't know how to do that in healthy ways. My task, as a Christian pastoral counselor, is to point them toward healthy ways to heal their pain and get their desires met. That starts with their willingness and the belief that only "living water," a relationship with Christ, will begin the journey of sobriety.

Every addict I work with will answer the three spiritual questions of this book. They will have to demonstrate to me that they are willing to give up old behaviors, know what they are really thirsty for, and begin to understand how to be selfless and not selfish. I believe that everything I've learned about helping addicts applies to everyone. If an addict can begin to live a life of integrity, so can anyone.

Selflessness is a rather large concept, don't you think? So I have long tried to figure out ways to help men understand it. This brings me back to the question, "What would you be willing to die for?" You see, most people can begin to at least think about that. Let's think about several possibilities.

Today, as I write, we have been fighting wars in Iraq and Afghanistan that are longer than any wars in United States history. Regularly we hear about casualties from those wars. We see stories about the families of those soldiers who have died, and we understand their pain. We recognize that those soldiers made the ultimate sacrifice. They were willing to die for their country. How about you?

I suppose your answer might depend on your age. I am a baby boomer, born between 1946 and 1964. We are the children of parents who came out of the Great Depression of the 1930s and then fought in World War II. My father was attached to the 101st Airborne Division, and Debbie's father was a pilot in Europe during and after the Normandy invasion. My dad is now dead, while Debbie's dad is very much alive and well at age ninety-one. In all the stories I ever heard either of them tell about those times, I never heard them raise any questions about serving their country. They are part of what the famous newscaster Tom Brokaw calls the Greatest Generation. They served and did what was asked of them, and many of them made the ultimate sacrifice.

This generation was indeed willing to die for their country. If you are in this generation, thank you. If you are a child or grandchild of that generation, have you ever told them how much you appreciate what they did?

If you are a baby boomer like me, what do you say about dying for your country? I feel a little guilty about that myself, because we lived during days of the Vietnam War and there were a lot of questions about serving your country. Let's not get into all the old questions about the justice of that war. Do some of you remember all the anxiety about how to avoid being drafted? There were some very creative strategies during those days, and the population of Canada got a little larger.

As for me, I was headed to seminary, and that was an automatic deferment in those days. Let me tell you that my seminary class contained some men who I'm sure were called less to the ministry and more to avoiding military service. There were those who did get drafted and did go to Vietnam, and fifty thousand made the ultimate sacrifice. Many more survived and came back, and many were never the same. Some of them still experience a great deal of trauma (called Post Traumatic Stress Syndrome or PTSD). What's worse, when they got home, they were generally reviled. Some were spit on and called various names, and that was an additional trauma. If you are one of those who served in that war, thank you.

More than likely, since I am old, you who are reading this are too young to remember all of this. I remember when one of my sons asked me about the Vietnam War because he was reading about it in a history textbook. I felt really old then. I'm sure, however, that everyone reading this book is old enough to remember 9/11. What a day that was, and all of us can remember where we were on that day. It seems to me that our whole attitude in this country changed that day. This was not a conflict in some foreign country. It was an attack on our nation. Do you remember how you felt? Were you not moved by the countless stories of the firefighters, the paramedics, the police, and even the parish priest who entered those buildings and lost their lives trying to help others?

You see, we are all moved to tears when we know about those who paid the price, who died for something. Did you not feel, after 9/11, however old you are, that you would be willing to confront terrorism and that you would be willing to sacrifice if called on to do so? Our whole patriotic attitude about our country and the military shifted that day. I was on a plane recently in which soldiers were coming back from Iraq or Afghanistan and heard the pilot announce to the whole plane that they were with us. The whole plane burst into spontaneous applause.

● KEY QUESTION

- Would you be willing to die for your country?

Let's keep this simple for the moment. How many of you reading this have children? I'm guessing that if I asked you if you'd be willing to die for any of them, your immediate response would be, "Of course!" You'd trade places with them if you could if they had a life-threatening disease. You'd step in front of an oncoming car. You'd donate a kidney. You'd do whatever it takes to keep them safe.

Would you do the same for a friend? Many people have made sacrifices because of friendship. Would you make sacrifices for a stranger? Remember those people who went into the World Trade Center after the planes hit. I'm sure they didn't know any of the people they wound up dying for. Jesus said something about this when he said that whatever we do or don't do for the least of people, we do or don't do for him (see Matt. 25:45).

Have I caused you to think? If so, now I want to ask what might be the hardest of questions: "Would you die for your spouse?" There may be some of you who answer, "Absolutely I would." Then others of you may respond, "Wait a minute! You don't know my spouse and what kind of a person she is. I'm not sure about your question." Even for those of you who said you would die for your spouse, how are you in fact treating that person?

We are called to pay the price for our spouse. In Paul's teaching to us about marriage in Eph. 5, he begins by saying, "Be imitators of God, therefore, as dearly loved children and live a life of love, just as Christ loved us and gave himself up for us as a fragrant offering and sacrifice to God" (vv. 1-2). Before we learn about serving each other later in the chapter, we must begin by being "imitators of God" with a childlike attitude. Love, then, is like the way Christ died for the church. That's a rather high calling. Remember in this life we are called to be imitators. None of us can be completely like Christ. It is an image to strive for with God's help. Men, how many of you have read this part later in the chapter: "Wives, submit to your husbands as to the Lord. For the husband is the head of the wife as Christ is the head of the church, his body, of which he is the Savior. Now as the church submits to Christ, so also wives should submit to their husbands in everything" (vv. 22-24). How many of you used it to make demands from your wife? Moreover, how many of you have not given attention to this verse that comes next: "Husbands, love your wives, just as Christ loved the church and gave himself up for her" (v. 25)?

Married men, we are called to be the head and we are called to be like Christ. We are not called to selfishly make demands or to feel like victims when our wives don't fulfill every one of our needs, desires, or thirsts.

⊛ KEY QUESTION

- Would you die for a child, a relative, a friend, or your spouse?

I also think of those many missionaries who go into very dangerous foreign situations. They are willing to die for their high calling to take the message of the gospel to all nations. Whether or not they think about it, they are really demonstrating a willingness to die for God's kingdom.

A willingness to die for someone or something is a willingness to sacrifice oneself. It is the highest form of selflessness and the polar opposite of selfishness. Now that you are thinking about sacrifice and selflessness, let's look at the story of Lazarus.

Mary, Martha, and Lazarus were siblings. We know very little of their family background. We do know they were from the village of Bethany, not far from Jerusalem and in Judea. In Luke 10:38-42 we learn that Jesus and his disciples came to their house and it is identified as Martha's, so we can assume that she was the oldest. In this passage we also learn that Martha was busy taking care of the house and that her sister Mary was sitting at Jesus' feet listening to him teach. Martha complains to Jesus that Mary is not helping and Jesus says to her, "'Martha, Martha,' the Lord answered, 'you are worried and upset about many things, but only one thing is needed. Mary has chosen what is better, and it will not be taken away from her'" (vv. 41-42). In modern parlance Jesus might say, "Don't sweat the small stuff." In short, the things of this world, such as a house, were not nearly as important as what he had to teach.

Martha does seem to be the more practical one, and Mary the more devoted one. It will be Mary that uses her own hair to anoint the feet of Jesus (John 12:3). Jesus must have spent some time with all three because we are told that Jesus loved all of them very much (11:5). The fact that Jesus loves them is mentioned several times in the story. Wouldn't you think, then, that if someone you loved was sick and his sisters sent you a message to come, you would come?

One of my favorite Sunday school songs from my youth is "What a Friend We Have in Jesus." How amazing it must have been to be great friends with Jesus as Lazarus, Martha, and Mary were. So, they send their friend a message that says, "The one you love is sick" (12:3). Jesus, however, decides to stay for two more days. He has already said, "This sickness will not end in death" (v. 4). He finally does decide to go back, but his disciples remind him that Judea is a dangerous place and that he has almost been stoned there (v. 8). Jesus replies with a teaching that those who walk in the light will not stumble as opposed to those who walk in darkness (vv. 9-10). I believe he is saying that we have to do what we have to do and that when we do, our path will be made straight. Earlier Jesus had said, "I am the light of the world. Whoever follows me will never walk in darkness, but will have the light of life" (8:12).

Jesus knows that Lazarus is dead and even says that he is glad he wasn't there so that the disciples might believe. He is setting the scene for the soon-to-come display of his resurrecting power. When he does get back, Jesus learns that Lazarus has already been in the tomb four days. Now Martha hears that Jesus is coming and she goes out to meet him. I wonder what the energy or the tone of her voice was when she says, "If you had been here, my brother would not have died" (11:21). Now Jesus has a conversation with her in which he says that Lazarus will rise again. Martha interprets this to mean that he will rise again on the last day, in other words, at the end of time (vv. 23-24).

Jesus responds with words we all know, "I am the resurrection and the life. He who believes in me will live, even though he dies; and whoever lives and believes in me will never die. Do you believe this?" (vv. 25-26). Do you begin to get the idea that this story is really about living eternally? Now it's Mary's turn to go out to see Jesus, and she says, "Lord, if you had been here, my brother would not have died" (v. 32).

Can you imagine the disappointment both of these sisters must feel at this point? Yes, they both believe in Jesus as the Messiah, and yes, they somewhat understand what he is saying about eternal life. But their brother is still dead. Have you ever had, like these sisters, any "if only" questions for Jesus? Have you believed yourself to be his friend and asked him to come at a time of great trouble for you? Have you, too, been disappointed that he didn't seem to come?

I know I have, and every day I talk to men who have those questions. Like me, these are usually men who have experienced consequences because of their sinful behavior. In many ways for them something has died—their jobs, their marriages, or their overall health. They have prayed to God, "Lord, I'm dying. Will you come and save me?" As they sit in their despair, they all have the anger of "if only." They ask, "Jesus, how can you be my friend when you didn't come?" Later in verse 37 other men are asking this exact question: "Could not he who opened the eyes of the blind man have kept this man from dying?"

When Mary brings her "if only" question to Jesus, she and others who came with her are weeping. Jesus is moved and greatly troubled and asks where they have laid Lazarus. They say they are going to show him and we have the shortest verse in the Bible, verse 35, "Jesus wept." Notice that in this story Jesus is teaching and demonstrating that he is the Messiah, the Light of the World, *and* yet he is human. Like the rest of them, he is sad. He feels the human emotion of love for a brother. Jesus, as we believe, is God in the flesh, possessing all the human feelings. Isn't it awesome that we have a Savior who knows how we feel and shares our pain? Wouldn't that explain Matthew's teaching that Jesus wants to be yoked with us and to share our burdens (Matt. 11:28-30). That is how they can become "light" (v. 30).

Mary, Martha, Jesus, and many others arrive at the tomb, and Jesus tells them to roll away the stone that covers it. Martha, the practical one, says, "By this time there is a bad odor, for he has been there four days" (John 11:39). She is saying, "We can't roll away the stone. He stinks." This is the second time in this story that Martha has questioned Jesus. Jesus corrects her again by explaining to her that if she only believed, she would see the glory of God (v. 40).

For any of you who have ever had a hard time believing, I want you to really understand that in this story a very rational woman, Martha, who is a friend of Jesus and who has seen him work miracles, is also a woman who has a hard time believing. Jesus has to correct her one more time.

So they roll away the stone. Jesus says loudly to Lazarus that he should "come out," and miraculously he does (vv. 43-44). Don't you love the last verse of this story when Jesus says, "Take off the grave clothes and let him go" (v. 44)?

Perhaps the reason I love this story so much is because there was a time when I thought I had died. Because of my sexual sins, my career certainly had, and I wasn't sure if Debbie would stay with me and whether our marriage had died. My story was in the local newspapers, and I thought any people who had liked me would certainly not like me now. My reputation had died. It seemed that my life, as I had known it, had come to an end. Like Martha, I had very practical thoughts of what was I going to do now. Given all of my guilt and shame, I certainly felt I "stunk." I remember it was then that I very clearly heard the voice of God telling me, "Mark, I'm not done with you yet." That message came to me simply when a friend reminded me of Paul's teaching in Phil. 1:6: "He who began a good work in you will carry it on to completion until the day of Christ Jesus."

When I began to hear and believe, I began to have hope. I still didn't have a job and still didn't know about my family, but there was hope. God wasn't done. So having destroyed a career, I cannot begin to tell you how God has continued to work in my life. Would I be sitting here writing a book if God had not resurrected my life? Not only is Debbie still here, but our relationship is more intimate than we had ever hoped. My kids still come around and occasionally mention how proud they are of me. Is that not a miracle?

Although God wasn't done with me back then, he did have a question: "Mark, are you willing to die to yourself?" He was saying to me, "Your problem is not just that you are addicted; your greater problem is that you have taken yourself too seriously. You have been too proud. You have spent too much time worrying about your career." It's as if he was saying he was going to allow all the consequences of my sin so that I could truly get broken, become humble, and come to depend on him. I had to die to myself, to my own fantasies, lies, pride, anger, and anxiety. At that time there was nowhere to go but up. I had to die to myself to find God.

The story of Lazarus is a story of resurrection. Jesus did nothing at first and let Lazarus die even though he greatly loved Lazarus. Jesus did this so that his power would be known by all, then and now.

Even though I knew that Jesus loved me and that he was my friend, I was really angry he didn't come sooner. I now know he really had to let me die so that his resurrecting power would also be known to me. God knew that my own arrogance and pride were in the way of what he really wanted to do with my life.

● KEY QUESTION

- Are you willing to die to yourself?

If you said yes, it is really important to know what needs to die in you. What are you holding on to that really needs to go? Let me suggest five aspects of your life to think about:

1. **Pride.** In the garden of Eden it was really Adam's and Eve's pride that tempted them to want to eat of the fruit of the tree of knowledge of good and evil. They did not trust God to totally take care of them. That original sin happened because God had created them with a free will to obey or disobey him. They chose to disobey, and we are all the inheritors of that sinful nature, a nature that is all about pride. Pride is the belief that we can do it alone and that we don't need God. It is an inability to trust.

2. **Arrogance.** This is a close cousin to pride. It is the belief that you are better than others. You don't need help and won't ask for it. Arrogance seeks to prove to others that you can do it alone and do it better. It is the feeling of being superior. What is most dangerous is that when you feel arrogance, you won't ask God or anyone else for help.

3. **Anger.** This is the feeling that someone has hurt you and perhaps that you want revenge. Anger grows out of sadness and pain and attempts to cover those feelings up by being mad at those who caused them. Sometimes you hold on to anger because you think if you let go of it, others will hurt you again. Anger and its cousin resentment give you a false feeling that you are powerful. Anger also allows you to think that you are entitled to get your needs and desires met in whatever way you can. It is rebellious and tempts you into even sinful acts because you think you deserve to do them. When you feel angry, you feel like a victim.

4. **Shame.** Shame has a set of core beliefs. You believe you are a bad and worthless person. You think no one will love you as you are. You worry no one will take care of you. You believe you are the only one who can take care of you. You often confuse shame with guilt. Guilt is, in fact, the knowledge that you make mistakes. Shame is the belief that you are a mistake. Shame causes you to believe the lie that not even God loves you. Shame is based on your real-life experience and is based on your history within your family and with friends. Shame can be the product of other people's sins against you.

5. **Anxiety.** This is the basic feeling that you are not safe. You have anxiety about health and dying, money, material things, doubts, and relationships. Anxiety causes you to think that you can control your health, your mon-

ey, your possessions, your beliefs, and all those you love around you. Anxiety leads to fears about many things. Fears, I believe, are smaller and more manageable. We have the ability to take large anxieties and "dumb them down" into smaller fears. You might, for example, be afraid of death, which is a large anxiety. Instead of thinking about death in general you pick out certain people and certain aspects of your life to try to control. You try to predict the future and imagine the worst. Then you seek to prepare for it. Anxiety causes you to be distracted by all the things you are worried about.

● KEY QUESTION

- Which of these five feelings do you think you experience the most in your life? (You might say one or all five.)

There are so many aspects of your life that these five feelings direct. These feelings have caused you to seek relief through so many false substitutes that really don't quench the thirst of your soul. These feelings may cause you to be stuck in a life of despair, emptiness, and loneliness. If you are willing to die to yourself, these are the core feelings you will need help with. They don't die easily. All I would ask in this book for now is that you are willing to work on them.

What do I mean by work on them? Here are several ideas:

- Tell someone about your decision. It might be a friend, a spouse, or some professional, such as a pastor or a counselor. Stay in dialogue with that person regularly.

- After you have broken your silence, which shame has kept you in, and stopped lying to yourself and others, there are perhaps false substitutes you will need to stop engaging in. You will need accountability to do so. The first book in this series, *The 7 Principles of Highly Accountable Men*, will guide you on how to be accountable.

- Seek spiritual direction. This could be someone you know who seems farther along in his or her spiritual journey. It might be a pastor or spiritual leader. Whoever it is, ask that person to hold you accountable to prayer, Scripture study, and meditation.

- Attend meetings, like twelve-step groups, where people regularly talk about their powerlessness, brokenness, and history of sin. These could also be church groups committed to changing something. The key is that each member will be able to talk about his or her story of sin and brokenness. Possibly this modeling by others will show you the path for yourself.

- If your sinful nature has created issues of mental illness or addiction in your life, seek professional Christian counseling. In the case of these problems, friends and spouses won't be enough to help you heal.

- Find people around you who seem to be examples of freedom from all the five unhealthy dynamics. These people will be calm, humble yet confident, sober, pure, and wise. Spend time with them whenever you can.

- Share your story with others. Become the person others who also seek to die to themselves will want to be with. By doing so, you will be giving back in ways that will also help you.

I don't want you to simply think you can read all of these suggestions and then be fine. All of what I've suggested will need a plan with action steps. Become a man of mighty vision. See yourself in the future and imagine what your life will be like. Then do whatever it takes, for as long as it takes. Finally, remember that this is a journey, as Alcoholics Anonymous says, of "progress rather than . . . perfection."[12] Don't beat yourself up if you don't always get it right, if you still make mistakes, and if you aren't always affirmed for the good things you are doing by those around you.

KEY QUESTION

- Read the following passage of Scripture first:

  Put to death, therefore, whatever belongs to your earthly nature: sexual immorality, impurity, lust, evil desires and greed, which is idolatry. Because of these, the wrath of God is coming. You used to walk in these ways, in the life you once lived. But now you must rid yourselves of all such things as these: anger, rage, malice, slander, and filthy language from your lips. Do not lie to each other, since you have taken off your old self with its practices and have put on the new self, which is being renewed in knowledge in the image of its Creator. (Col. 3:5-10)

  ○ How does this passage pertain to you today?

○ What do you think God is saying to you through these words?

○ What action step can you take today to practice putting something to death?

At the end of this chapter, my prayer for you is that you come to a place of deep surrender, a place of dying to yourself. May you then experience the peace of letting God control your life, and may you be resurrected like Lazarus, not physically, but spiritually in ways you can't even imagine.

CONCLUSION—YOUR ANSWERS WILL MAKE A DIFFERENCE

I promised to ask you three spiritual questions and along the way have asked you so many more. I hope you have been able to digest all of them without too much struggle. If you did take time to think, pray, journal, and share with others, I pray that at the close of this book you can say you are a person who has grown spiritually and emotionally. I believe if you can, it will make a difference in the world.

Margaret Mead, the great anthropologist of the twentieth century, studied cultures all over the world. I once heard the great preacher Tony Evans talk about her, and he said that what she observed is how people and cultures change. Dr. Mead believed, he said, that it is not armies, power, or force that creates change. It is not wealth or the accumulation of material things either. Rather, she said, according to Evans, it is one person changing his or her life and thereby changing a family, then a community, and then a nation, and then the world. What a grand idea that is!

What is important about Dr. Mead's idea is not that you can change the world but that maybe the world can change if more people will do as you and change themselves. Are you willing to be whole? Are you willing to give up your thirst for unhealthy solutions and be thirsty for living water? Are you willing to die to yourself? If you answer yes to each of these questions, you will be the man of integrity and honor God calls you to be.

Jesus tells us that the greatest commandment is to love God "with your heart and with all your soul and with all your mind" (Matt. 22:37). "And," he says, "the second is like it, 'Love your neighbor as yourself'" (v. 39). Those of you who have read my second book in this series, *Taking Every Thought Captive,* know that I have a lot to say about this commandment. For now, and in conclusion, let me tell you my firm belief that answering yes to all of the three spiritual questions is the deepest way to truly love God and love yourself. Then, according to Jesus, you will be able to love others.

If you can love others, then my prayer is that you will encounter these things:

- You will notice around you the smiles of those you love.
- You will experience others who want to give back to you.
- You will find things that used to totally bother you won't do so anymore.
- You will feel love more deeply.
- You will experience a new level of friendship and community than you have ever known before.
- You will be more productive in all you do.
- You will develop a mighty vision of God's calling in your life.

- You will give and sacrifice for others in ways you never thought possible.
- And you will know what Paul says is the "peace . . . which passeth all understanding" (Phil. 4:7, KJV).

May the love, grace, and peace of God keep your hearts and minds in Christ Jesus. Amen.

NOTES

1. *Merriam-Webster,* s.v. "integrity," http://www.merriam-webster.com/dictionary/integrity (accessed May 11, 2011).

2. *Merriam-Webster,* s.v. "integer," http://www.merriam-webster.com/dictionary/integer (accessed May 11, 2011).

3. *Blue Letter Bible,* s.v. "hygiēs," http://www.blueletterbible.org/lang/lexicon/lexicon.cfm?Strongs=G5199&t=KJV (accessed June 27, 2011).

4. Ibid.

5. See "Bill's Story," chap. 1 in *The Big Book Online,* Alcoholics Anonymous World Services, http://www.aa.org/bigbookonline/en_bigbook_chapt1.pdf (accessed May 11, 2011). See also *Wikipedia,* s.v. "Bill W.," http://en.wikipedia.org/wiki/Bill_W (accessed May 11, 2011).

6. See William Barclay, *The Gospel of John,* vol. 1, The Daily Study Bible, 2nd ed. (Philadelphia: Westminster Press, 1956), 137-43.

7. In this and all other stories, I never use the real name of a person, and in some cases, the stories are fictional but representative of actual people.

8. Alcoholics Anonymous, "The Twelve Steps of Alcoholics Anonymous," http://www.aa.org/en_pdfs/smf-121_en.pdf (accessed April 8, 2011).

9. Helen Fisher, *Why We Love* (New York: Henry Holt, 2004).

10. Mark and Debbie Laaser, *The Seven Desires of the Heart* (Grand Rapids: Zondervan, 2009).

11. See my second book in this series, *Taking Every Thought Captive,* particularly the chapter on fantasy if you want to learn more about it.

12. "How It Works," chap. 5 in *The Big Book Online,* 60, Alcoholics Anonymous World Services, http://www.aa.org/bigbookonline/en_bigbook_chapt5.pdf (accessed May 11, 2011).

RESOURCES

One of the dynamics I have observed over the years is how often contact information, Web sites, and the availability of books change. We are living in an electronic age and so much of what we read is on the Internet. So rather than list books or articles that I find helpful, I encourage you to stay in touch with the most recent material by regularly checking Web sites or doing Internet searches for information relevant to your needs.

There are two Web sites that will most likely continue to be current:

1. Our Web site is www.faithfulandtrueministries.com. On it you will find articles, videos, references to helpful books, and other counseling resources. A calendar of our workshops and speaking engagements throughout the country are included as well. We also provide, without charge, general education to the public through Web-based seminars, or Webinars. We will likewise be offering training Webinars for professionals, such as pastors and counselors, with the possibility, in some cases, of participants earning CEUs. Lectures by Debbie, other colleagues, and myself will also be archived on this site. Material from this book series will at times be presented as well.

2. Another Web site is www.aacc.net. This is the site of the American Association of Christian Counseling. The AACC is the largest association of Christian counselors in the world. This site has a directory of counselors in your area. You will also find on this site several video training series on a number of topics. It is possible to get trained as a lay counselor or certified in several areas as a professional counselor by using these video courses. Some of those video series include Debbie and me. The AACC also conducts large national and international conferences that are a joy to attend. It is the best place to network with colleagues and friends. So stay in touch with what they are doing.

When lost in the maze of the Web, please call or email us directly. I, Debbie, or one of our staff will get back to you with specific questions. We enjoy pointing people in the right direction.

Mark R. Laaser, MDiv, PhD
Debbie Laaser, MA
Faithful and True Ministries, Inc.
15798 Venture Lane
Eden Prairie, MN 55344
952-746-3880
mlaaser@faithfulandtrueministries.com
dlaaser@faithfulandtrueministries.com
www.faithfulandtrueministries.com